Praise for *Team Renaissance:*

"For possibilities to become reality, you need a leader who can effectively mix together a dream, tenacity, intuition, intellectual curiosity, listening skills, consumer needs and action orientation. Unfortunately, the road is littered with possibilities that were never fully realized because the leader was unable to lead a team effectively toward his or her dream. Team Renaissance will give you the formula to become the Chief Possibilities Officer of your company — no matter your level in the organization."

Aimee Golden Johnson
Vice President Starbucks Card, Loyalty, Segmentation and Customer Journey

"I have shelves of books dedicated to the topics found in *Team Renaissance*. The beauty of this particular book is that it takes those subjects, distills them down to the essentials, and presents them in one volume in a well-organized and very visually appealing manner. The authors also know the value of storytelling and share stories of people we know (and some we don't, but wish we did) that are easy to remember and that you'll want to repeat. The personal assessments, quick tips, and quotes that are interspersed throughout make for a read that is as enjoyable as it is instructive. Read this to improve, inspire and invigorate your team — and yourself."

Mart Martin, Brand Strategist
Jackson Spalding Marketing & Public Relations, Atlanta, Georgia

"I love that this book presents team building and leadership skills in the context of storytelling. Besides bringing clarity to the muddy waters of management, it offers real-life stories about beating the odds such as the story of Dmitri Mendeleev, who invented the periodic table, or Drew Brees, when he decided to join the New Orleans Saints post-Katrina or Elmer Foster, who invented the time-keeping scoreboard. Poignantly written, these stories weaved throughout illustrate beautifully that team building and getting the job done — and done right — is not just about business plans and strategic workshops. It's about listening to ____ and interacting with them. I highly recommend it."

Juli Metzger, former Editor
Indianapolis Star

"We all work in teams. *Team Renaissance* provides the framework to build a high-performing team culture. This is the best book on the subject in years."

William D. Toler, President/CEO

AdvancePierre Foods

"Timely, insightful, and a comprehensive approach to leveraging teams in today's dynamic environment. The *Team Arch*® is particularly innovative because it provides a comprehensive framework for creating synergy within teams without prescribing invasive rules and structures. I really like the *Team Arch*® because it seems to strip away a lot of unnecessary "team building" busy work and refocuses efforts on meaningful, day-to-day activities which leaders can use to optimize team performance. "

Geoffrey T. Stewart, Ph.D.

Moody College of Business Administration
University of Louisiana

"*Team Renaissance: The Art, Science and Politics of Great Teams* is a common-sense approach to all that ails business and businesses today. The language and anecdotes are clean and concise and are easily applied to any place of business. The exercises are meaningful and easy to understand. They're also a good, strong road map for any organization to follow. Too often, businesses get mired in the day-to-day and don't pay enough attention to efficiency, transparency and culture. The first 10 chapters do all of that and more."

Lee Ivory, former Editor

Baseball Weekly

"A focus on team-building and team creativity certainly strikes the right chord in a collaborative-driven era that is about as far-removed from the "lone ranger" approach exemplified in TV's Mad Men as can be. Even the format should appeal to a rising generation of leaders accustomed to multi-tasking, visual vivacity (what in the old days would have been called "busy" layout). The authors offer solid advice on preparing for a team project, setting goals and measurables, and in providing — an often forgotten element in management tomes — good examples for the team-skeptical on how to keep the process on-track and productive."

Gene Policinski, Senior Vice President/Executive Director

First Amendment Center, former Sports Editor at USA TODAY

TEAM

RENAISSANCE

THE ART, SCIENCE & POLITICS OF GREAT TEAMS

RICHARD SPOON & JAN RISHER
WITH CONTRIBUTIONS BY JESSE EDELMAN & STEPHEN PEELE

OLD MAN RIVER
PUBLISHING

OLD MAN RIVER
PUBLISHING

Team Renaissance®: The Art, Science and Politics of Great Teams
Copyright ©2012 by Richard Spoon and Jan Risher.
Team Renaissance and the Team Arch are registered trademarks of Old Man River Publishing®.

Special discounts on bulk quantities of Old Man River Publishing® books are available to corporations, professional associations and other organizations. For details, contact the Director of Book Sales at Old Man River Publishing®.

www.oldmanriverpublishing.com

Edited by Dale Irwin and Arnessa Garrett
Cover art by Giovanni Auriemma with reference to Michelangelo's Piazza del Campidoglio in Rome.
Book design and illustrations by WORKagencies, workagencies.com
Photograph of Richard Spoon by Shokare Nakpodia | Photograph of Jan Risher by Tim Landry
Printed in China

Visit www.teamrenaissance.net for more information.

Requests for information should be addressed to:
Old Man River Publishing®, Lafayette, Louisiana 70508

Spoon, Richard, 1963 –
Team Renaissance®: The Art, Science and Politics of Great Teams / Richard E. Spoon & Jan Risher
ISBN : 978-1-938222-01-6 (paperback)

1. Teams in the workplace 2. Motivating Teams 3. Decision-making, Group

SECOND EDITION - March 2014

To our children:

Archer Jordan

Gentry

Gerald Evan

Greer

Jackson

Lilian

Logan Elliott

Micaiah Victoria

Paulena Claire

Piper

Samantha

Stephen Jr.

Contents

CHAPTER 6: Defined Roles — 89

CHAPTER 7: Sharp Insights — 103

CHAPTER 8: Relevant Rewards 121

CHAPTER 9: Consistent Communication 139

Acknowledgements of authors and contributors

There are so many people who are a part of this book, but my biggest lessons in teamwork and life have come from my wife, Rachel, who entered my world 20 years ago this year and changed everything for the better. She embodies the spirit of teamwork. Without her unmovable support, this project could not have been completed. I want to thank the tireless mentors who have positively impacted my professional career and made me a better team leader. Many of the insights in this book came from practical field testing with fellow teammates at Procter & Gamble and the Campbell Soup Company through the 1980s and 1990s. I learned dedication and commitment from my high school football team (Odessa Permian/GO MOJO!) — most notably Russell Ray, Steve Strifler and our head coach John Wilkins. My dad, Marvin Spoon, coached most of my baseball teams growing up and reminded me regularly, "This team is only as strong as its weakest link. Together, we can off-set our individual weaknesses. Now, go out there and play as one team." Finally, I want to thank my co-author and contributors, and particularly Jan Risher for her patience, focus and commitment to push through long nights and weekends to help us find our voice.

-Richard Spoon

I would like to thank the two most important "team players" in my life, my wife Tara Lynn Peele, and my mother Cynthia Constance Peele. I believe their example of strong servant leadership has not only helped me do what I needed to do but taught me how to do it with greater sensitivity and empathy.

-Stephen Peele

Back in 1980, Donna McLean, junior English teacher at Magee High in Magee, Mississippi, taught me to write. In doing so, she changed my life. Thanks to her and other great teachers who told me stories and taught me to think—including Ovid Vickers, Nancy Chambers, the late Frances Thompson and my mom, Nelda Risher, who was also my fourth grade reading teacher. Throughout my formative years, my dad, Gary Risher, coached a string of high school football teams that won all the games necessary to cement my positive outlook on life. (Go Bearcats!) Thanks to Tanya Dobbs Crawley, Gail Stubbs Chancellor, Sophia Smith Daldine, Sondra Wash and Louise Pierce for being great teammates long ago. Juli Metzger, Marsha Sills, Kayla Gagnet Castille, Arnessa Garrett, Claudia Laws, Tim Landry and Ben Leger taught me the value of getting the details right. They also reinforced the value of the human connection and teamwork—especially when working under tough circumstances. Thanks to Elizabeth Lyons, Sloan Lamotte, Lindsay Dreher, Stacey Chamberlain, Jillian Johnson and Bram Johnson for their attention to detail and vision for this project. I thank Richard Spoon for his wisdom and faith in seeing this project to fruition. Lastly, thanks to Julio Naudin, my husband. He steadfastly lifts the people around him. I am grateful to have been one of those people for more than 20 years. He has changed my world for the good.

-Jan Risher

I would like to thank my wife, Lisa, for all her amazing support over the last 16 years. She is the most amazing wife and mother I know. She makes it possible for me to do the work I love so much. I would also like to thank my late father, Lennie Edelman, for always showing me that the easiest path might not always be the best one for you, and to my late mother, Yolanda Edelman, for showing me how family is like a 3- legged stool—it can support you, but if you lean on it too hard, it'll break. Finally, I would like to acknowledge those people that have influenced me over my career, including Mike Graen, Lee Rodriguez, Joe Soules and, the person who believed in me from day one, Richard Spoon.

-Jesse Edelman

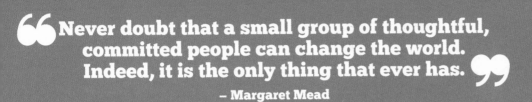

Building Blocks

At the base of Abraham Maslow's hierarchy of needs are the physiological requirements for staying alive—breathing, food, water. The next strata of the pyramid addresses safety—security of body, health and resources.

And after these basic needs are met, the third element in the hierarchy of what motivates human beings is the need for building relationships with others and belonging. People seek the human connection. They seek meaning. They want to belong to something they're proud of, something that offers definition to their identity through their sheer association with it. Great teams provide this framework.

1.2 Everybody has a story

Anybody who has ever been a part of a schoolyard pick knows that simply because a group of people are called a team does not mean they are truly a team. It does not mean that all or any of the team members feel like they belong.

Whether in a Fortune 500 corporation or a smaller group, everybody on a team would like to belong and feel needed for what they contribute to the cause. They'd like to move beyond the day-to-day grind to a place where creativity and meaning connect them. They'd like to reach a place where they and all their teammates choose to volunteer their experience—their existence on the team. That's belonging.

The essence of belonging gets at the heart of why so many people like to refer back to their high school or college days. Much of high school and college is designed to promote team behavior and give students the chance to find their niche and a place to belong. For too many, those good old days turn out to be the only time in their lives when they had the chance to be part of a true team. They tell and relive their glory-day stories because when they look back, they know when they were most connected to other people—it was when they worked in teams.

When organizations become so focused on the final work product that they forget to value teams and team identities, they lose out. They miss out on the possibilities of greatness those teams could achieve—as opposed to organizations comprising individuals and haphazard groupings of disengaged people who are, at best, defined by the work they do.

Teams that reach that productive plane get past simply coming together to produce a good or service. They come together to cheat the universe and build something meaningful.

1.3 The most powerful weapon on earth

Business leaders and managers have to remember that work has the potential to be a place that nurtures employees' passions and lights a fire in their souls. When that happens, productivity and innovation skyrocket. As Ferdinand Foch said, "The most powerful weapon on earth is the human soul on fire."

Large organizations spend a great deal of time and energy making agreements and training employees in an effort to improve the ways people operate at work. However, organizations can't train people to be open or fair or responsible if the real agreement is that the organization will win at all costs. Training programs will never resolve that disconnect— behaviors change when people decide to belong together differently.

No organization, regardless of its size, has the wherewithal to harness the human spirit, but teams and the connection they offer have the potential to make individuals better. Each person seeks to achieve more as a part of a group. Feeling connected makes each individual feel worthy and a part of something great. Think of all the stories of people who have been on great teams. The experience is life-changing—and the people who lived it tell the stories for years. The experience becomes a part of the person. It plays a key role in defining who that person is. That person belonged to a team. It may have been a sports team, but it didn't have to be. It could have been drama, debate, the marching band or the yearbook staff. Whatever it was, when someone was a member of a genuine team, the experience made them grow as an individual and turned them into a different and better person.

People's lives are meaningful when they move toward each other and build relationships.

1.4 Building blocks of organizations

Great companies are almost always made great by a few small teams. Some people might say it was their corporate strategy that made the difference. Others may say it was their corporate research. But most people on the inside would say it was a team of committed individuals who believed they could create something that would fundamentally change how people worked—and their spirit and vision which spread, first throughout the company itself and then into the marketplace.

In essence, teams are the building blocks of the most successful organizations. The best teams complement one another and inspire. The smaller groups connect to form a larger system. Activities are linked; commerce is produced. The connectivity between the teams and the people on the teams make companies successful.

1.5 Stripping away

Through the 1990s and the first decade of the 2000s, corporations stripped away both time and resources that once ensured that the organization worked effectively. Organizations have flattened. The result is managers, employees and the organization at large have a greater need to develop competency in how to work in and lead teams.

During the dotcom bust and subsequent financial meltdowns, corporations stripped out multiple levels of management and increased span of control, adding pressure onto the system—which is designed to limit the human connection. In fact, many corporate cultures are defined by how busy people are. Being overly busy leads to islands and a lack of connectivity in the workplace. More and more in organizations, the breakdown occurs in individuals stretched too thin, adding an extra helping of pressure on the human connection.

1.6 Making teams work

Focusing on the team is about getting back to the basics of what makes an organization work. If the bottom line is money, focusing on teams is not going to cost any more (and may even save money) in the short and long run. Plus, an investment in teams will produce significantly better results and make happier people.

If an organization wants to raise the bar on performance, then it has to create an environment where people can creatively solve problems. In teams, the voyage will assuredly be messy, but collaboratively, the team will eventually decipher the challenges in ingenious ways.

People work together on teams to achieve greatness for the organization, but what makes teams work? To be effective, teams must rely on and uphold a few basic principles. For example, team members need to know and understand the team's clear direction and practices. They must communicate, and they need a strong leader. Their roles, rewards and measures must be well defined.

To succeed, teams require attention to the very basics organizations have stopped emphasizing. Creating and nurturing effective teams require getting back to the fundamentals of good solid management. Great teams work and produce because of the human connection. People yearn to work together.

Companies pay for employees to perform activities and tasks, but employees volunteer their creativity. Teams create an environment where people choose to do just that—to become engaged and contribute their best ideas to the company. Team members want to be involved.

Happier people work harder.

1.7 Harvesting the fruits of teams

Spending time on teams doesn't cost a lot of money and can produce incredible results. However weird it may seem, there's a great analogy between growing teams and growing tomato plants. First, you have to plant—and plant deep. Few leisure gardeners know that growing a tomato plant requires digging a hole almost as deep as the plant is high. For example, to plant a 12-inch high tomato plant in a four-inch pot, a gardener should dig a hole about 14 inches deep—and plant the whole plant, roots, stem, leaves and all, leaving about two inches peeking through the soil.

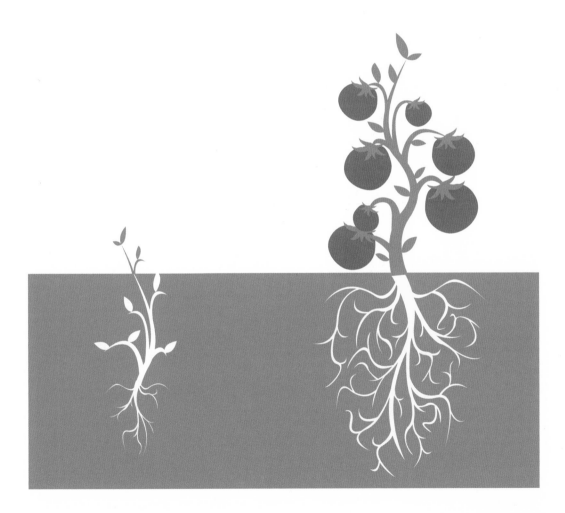

Then the gardener has to nurture those little tomato plants with deep roots with all the nutrients and water and sunlight the need. The nurturing stage lasts a while—and during that critical period the gardener gets little in return, other than exercise.

But lo and behold, that plant starts growing. It grows so much that it requires support. Before it produces fruit, even the healthiest of tomato plants can't hold themselves up.

Finally, with much time, effort and commitment, the tomato plant begins to flourish and will produce fruit well into the season. The gardener will reap the benefits of his or her effort tenfold. All because he or she did the work on the frontend.

Producing great teams requires the same kind of work and dedication. A team grower has to have a deep understanding of a team's needs and the motivations of its members. The team grower has to dig deep before the team is ever planted.

Then, the grower has to nurture—and nurturing comes in a variety of forms. A tomato plant with too much sunlight and not enough water will not thrive. Neither will one with too much water and not enough sunlight. Even if a plant has proper sunlight and water, but is planted in poor soil with no additional nutrients, the plant will produce little to no fruit. In fact, the plant may very well shrivel and die.

Like a tomato plant, even if the team gets all the nurturing it needs, that may not be enough. Without proper support as the plant begins to grow, it will not thrive. It cannot support itself and may bend or break. However, with all the right groundwork in place, the team and the plant will produce fruit—and lots of it.

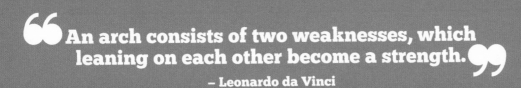

> **An arch consists of two weaknesses, which leaning on each other become a strength.**
> – Leonardo da Vinci

Go Team!

People like putting abstract concepts and ideas into orderly groups.

Back in the 1860s while the Americans were busy with less civil matters, many scientists across Europe were working to figure out and give order to the earth's most basic elements. At least six scientists in five countries—Germany, Italy, France, England and Russia—played critical roles in organizing the elements by weight and eventually developing the periodic table.

Dmitri Mendeleev earned the lion's share of the credit for inventing the periodic table after a rough and tumble start at life in Siberia. He was the youngest of at least 14 children. His mother started a glass factory after his father went blind and could no longer support the family. Then as he was finishing high school, his father died and his mother's glass factory burned to the ground. However, Mendeleev's mom was determined her youngest son would get a college education. So she took Dmitri to St. Petersburg and worked determinedly to get him into college. She succeeded.

By the time Mendeleev turned 40, he had arranged the 63 known elements by their atomic weights and organized the elements into groups possessing similar properties. He created the periodic table. Once he had the elements organized, he realized gaps existed between some elements. He used the gaps to predict elements that eventually would be discovered. He went so far as to predict the gap elements' properties.

He was right.

He developed an orderly graphic illustration that has led to untold discoveries. Three of the *gap* elements he predicted were found in his lifetime and provided strong evidence for his table to become the eventual keystone for chemistry. Though his creation didn't change anything about the way the universe works, it has provided an understanding for how the universe is put together.

Like Mendeleev's thoughts about the earth's building blocks, the Team Arch® provides a comprehensive framework on collective thinking about building great teams to remind people that teams and teamwork are still important.

The Team Arch® doesn't claim to bring a new order to the universe, but it does claim to order how the chief building block of companies and organizations works.

2.2
The Team Arch®

Just as the arch provides support for a structure, teams act as the foundation for any successful organization. Individual pieces hold the arch together, uniting to form a design that allows for the equal distribution of weight across the entire structure. Applying this concept, the Team Arch® identifies nine performance characteristics that consistently build exceptional teams.

2.3 Clear Direction

In the Team Arch®, Clear Direction sits in the keystone position of the model.

In an architectural arch, the keystone locks all the stones in place and allows the arch to bear weight. Clear Direction serves a similar purpose for teams—it locks team members together. It's the reason the team exists regardless of the industry or type of team. Every team member has to understand the group's core objectives and goals. Without that known alignment, a team will never achieve its full potential.

Occasionally, teams understand and are aligned to a definite and clear direction from the start. But when they're off—even marginally early on, the further the team goes, the further off course they may end up. However, even when teams know exactly where they want to go, they still have to form a cohesive approach on which route to take to get there.

Building great teams takes time. The teams have to learn to buffer the bumps along the road to maintain focus on the clear direction.

Chapter 3, Clear Direction, focuses on:

1. Setting direction. To create and maintain a clear direction, everyone on the team must understand the mission.

2. Planning. The team needs to have a clearly defined approach and action plan to achieve the mission.

3. Aligning. Teams must galvanize around the mission and the action required.

4. Capabilities. The team's goals must be reasonable with respect to the team's capabilities.

5. Priorities. The team has to know and embrace the top priorities.

6. Resources. The team must have the resources to get the job done.

7. Measures. While working together, the team needs to know how success is defined.

8. Reflection. The team should consistently review and revise priorities based on its performance.

2.4 Common Measures

Shared measurements of performance define success for the whole team and give the team the ability to track progress toward the goal.

A scorecard is designed to keep critical measures visible to the team. Successful scorecards require data that is accessible and easy to validate. Using the scorecard effectively results in increased transparency. It distributes ownership from the leader to the team, making team members openly accountable for their parts.

For a scorecard to be effective, it must be updated and reviewed regularly. When scores don't get posted for the entire team to consider, team members can get lulled into a false sense of success. Additionally, like a scoreboard at a sports event, the scorecard is an ever-present reminder that time is ticking. Without the score and the element of time, a team loses a sense of urgency.

Chapter 4, Common Measures, focuses on:

1. Defining measures. The team has a scorecard that tracks performance.

2. Transparency. The team's scorecard is visible to all.

3. Accountability. Team members have clear individual performance measures.

4. Ease. A team's measures are easy to track and validate.

5. Timeliness. The team's scorecard is monitored regularly—weekly, monthly and annually.

6. Management routine. The team has a regular review of the scorecard and based on progress, adjustments are made to the plan.

7. Self-regulation. Everyone on the team takes ownership when it comes to reviewing and delivering the measures.

8. Urgency. The scorecard instills a sense of urgency for the team.

2.5 Efficient Practices

Creating efficient practices ensures the team runs effectively.

Common team practices include meetings, planning, problem solving, communication and hand-offs. Many team practices are interrelated. A breakdown in one could lead to a breakdown in another, resulting in confusion and contributing to conflict. This combination may cause a team to lose focus and momentum, hampering achievement overall.

Left unattended, workflow takes the path of least resistance—and goes directly to the people who will get the job done, rather than an even, logical or more productive distribution. The result is an unfair mix of overworked and underworked team members.

Improving a team practice requires discipline and sometimes a dismantling of the status quo. On the strongest teams, work practices are regularly considered, streamlined and made efficient.

Chapter 5, Efficient Practices, focuses on:

1. Planning Horizons. The team has an effective approach to planning both short and long-term.

2. Prioritizing. The team has a clear process to identify and manage priorities.

3. Resource allocation. The team is effective at resource planning and making necessary adjustments based on changing priorities.

4. Core work processes. The team has key work processes that are well defined, written and practiced.

5. Meetings. Team members consider meetings both effective (we get stuff done) and efficient (we're mindful of time as a critical resource).

6. Problem solving. The team is successful at defining the problem, identifying root cause, clarifying options and making decisions.

7. Hand-offs. Hand-offs between team members and others outside the team are clear and well managed.

8. Continuous improvement. The team regularly reviews and consistently improves business practices.

9. Communication. The team's communication process can be defined as open, direct, timely and accurate.

10. Conflict resolution. The team has an effective approach to managing conflict both internally and with others outside the team.

2.6 Defined Roles

A successful team breaks down the work so clearly that each team member fully understands his or her responsibilities and the consequences if the defined tasks are not completed.

The team leader must delineate the tasks, according to capabilities, competencies and capacity. Team members know that they each have a place on the team—and that place is of value.

Having the right people in the right roles allows for one of the great ironies in organization design: the majority of decisions being made at the lowest level possible—not pushed up to a great and visionary leader or a team of anointed executives. Decisions made at the lowest level possible by competent team members, closest to the work, usually make the most sense.

Chapter 6, Defined Roles, focuses on:

1. Defined responsibilities. Each team member understands his or her job responsibilities.

2. Big picture. The team members understand how their work links with other team members and work processes.

3. Ownership. Each team member takes responsibility for getting the work done—or not.

4. Competency. The team has the right skills to accomplish its goals.

5. Leverage. The team fully utilizes the skills, knowledge and experience of team members.

6. Clear expectations. The team leader clearly sets work expectations for each team member.

7. Decision rights. Team members know the decisions they should make and the decisions others should make.

8. Decision level. Decisions are made at the appropriate level in the organization.

9. Regulated and balanced. Team members' roles and workload are regularly reviewed, prioritized and balanced, in accordance with team goals.

2.7 Sharp Insights

Good insight drives team action. Effective teams pull out insightful nuggets from data and move on.

If not, they get stuck in analysis paralysis. Successful teams are capable of bringing data to life. To turn data into useful insights, a team needs a clear understanding of the situation and its moving parts, including how the data was gathered and what weaknesses the data may have. A team has to know that history is going to repeat itself unless they do something fundamentally different.

The sheer volume of information accessible to anyone able to use the Internet highlights the difference between information and insights. Even with worldwide access to more data than ever before, a team must be interested and willing to tinker.

Reaching real insights requires a genuine curiosity and a willingness to dig.

Chapter 7, Sharp Insights, focuses on:

1. Analytical skills. The team has the analytical skills to turn data into useful insights.

2. Productivity. A team is able to analyze information quickly and efficiently.

3. Increased clarity. The team's planning process is enhanced by the effective use of information.

4. Mining the data. The team is capable of gathering and interpreting data.

5. Joyful capabilities. The team is designed with a blend of analytical skills and contentment with the work.

6. Quality decisions. A team's decision-making is rooted in sufficient data and insights.

7. Moving forward. A team avoids analysis paralysis and pushes forward through inevitable information gaps.

2.8 Relevant Rewards

Organizations reward the behavior they want repeated.

Rewards can be organized in three groups: recognition, responsibility and compensation. While the competitive nature of reward is important, being careful not to overly recognize individual performance over team performance is critical. Untangling conflicting and layered employee objectives will help an organization make the most meaningful and beneficial rewards choices. Teams must keep recognitions and rewards fresh and relevant.

Earning and offering rewards is an opportunity for team leaders, team members and organizations at large to give employees the chance to realize meaningful connections with other people. Those human connections tend to be the most memorable rewards team members earn at work. Employee rewards not only benefit the employees, but they can also have a positive impact on the employer across the board.

Chapter 8, Relevant Rewards, focuses on :

1. Recognition. Team members value and regularly recognize both individual and team performance.

2. Accountability. Team members hold each other accountable for delivering results.

3. Framework. The team has a formal rewards program that is transparent and consistent.

4. Impact. Rewards directly impact team performance.

5. Compensation. Team members believe they receive a fair balance of compensation, benefits, incentives and rewards for their work.

6. Linking values. The team leader recognizes and rewards examples of team members who live the team's stated values.

7. Appreciation. Team members feel valued for their contributions.

8. Consequences. Poor performance earns fair and deliberate consequences.

9. Human connections. The team is rewarded with and takes the time to make real human connections.

2.9 Consistent Communication

Trust and open communication are the leading components of collaboration.

Teams can put up with a lack of trust for a while and still get the work done. However, if trust continues to erode, the team's dynamics steadily become more and more dysfunctional. Sometimes little things add up to destroy trust. A team member is consistently late to meetings. A team member rarely completes a project on time. A team member doesn't return calls or emails. Other times, more blatant breaches occur and eat away at trust—thereby tearing down any interest in collaboration.

One of the most basic success factors of collaboration is the ability and willingness to give and receive feedback—part of creating constructive feedback is the courage to give it, and part of it is the courage to receive it. How a team gives and receives feedback relates to trust. If all components of trust are missing, collaboration can't happen. However, if a team is made up of capable, competent people, whether they're trustworthy or not, the work will still get done. The work may be painful and inefficient, but it will get done. Without competent people, a team won't succeed. Without people of character, a team will waste time, energy and resources. Success may come, but the team won't last.

Chapter 9, Consistent Collaboration, focuses on:

1. **Open expression.** Team members are encouraged to express themselves openly and honestly.

2. **Who does what.** Team members are able to declare what each does for the team.

3. **Feedback.** Team members seek input and constructive feedback from each other on their performance.

4. **Taking responsibility.** Each team member accepts responsibility for getting the work done.

5. **Mastery.** Each team member does his or her job with excellence.

6. **Encouraging dissent.** Team members challenge each other about plans and approaches.

7. **Intent.** Team members trust one another's motives and commitment.

8. **Character.** Team members trust each other not to intentionally harm the team.

9. **Staying informed.** Team members create, share and receive regular progress updates both within and outside the team.

2.10 Solid Culture

Organizational culture is the shared values and behaviors that contribute to the unique social and psychological environment of an organization–the personality of the place.

The team has to find a natural resting place inside the organization's culture. If the team's objective and goals require it to create a different culture than the company has, then the team has to be aware of the challenges of interacting with the other culture. If a team fights an organization's culture too much, the organization will alienate it and impact its ability to be effective. The most successful teams find the balance.

The challenge comes when an organization or a team realizes the need for a change in culture. Leaders must first define and delineate the existing culture and understand the relationship between culture and performance. Without an alteration of the fundamental goals, values and expectations, change remains superficial and short-term. Solid culture is at the base of the Team Arch®. In architectural terms, the base supports the entire arch. A weak base yields an arch that won't withstand difficulties and is bound to fall.

Chapter 10, Solid Culture, focuses on:

1. Stating values. The team has a written set of values that guides behavior.

2. Living values. The team walks the talk related to stated values.

3. Customer focus. The team focuses on delivering customer expectations, both internal and external.

4. Rituals. The team takes the time to celebrate good performance, team transitions and meaningful personal events.

5. Sense of urgency. The team considers time to be a critical resource.

6. Conflict management. The team manages conflict through open and forthright communication.

7. Conflict resolution. The team takes a pro-active stance on solving conflict by focusing on the facts versus opinions.

8. Dignity and respect. Team members treat one another with respect.

9. Civility. The team exhibits conduct that demonstrates courtesy, politeness and civility.

10. Diversity. The team's diverse skills, experience and perspectives enhance their ability to work effectively.

2.11 Team Leader

Though great leaders use a variety of leadership styles, they universally draw wisdom from experience–their own and that of others.

Regardless of the field, great leaders capitalize on the value of experience—the chance to recognize what works and what doesn't. The best leaders find common threads of achievements. They refine and build upon triumphs. They learn from failures. They grow. Leaders who continue to succeed listen, retain sufficient humility and remember whom they serve.

Architectually, the team leader's position on the Team Arch® is called the *abacus*. It's the piece of stone that juts out from the arch's columns and largely supports the weight of the arch itself. Like the abacus, leaders too must be willing to take positions where and when they stand alone. In doing so, they bear the weight of the team.

Chapter 11, Team Leader, focuses on:

1. Clear direction. A team leader ensures that a team is focused on the objective, has common buy-in and understands its shared vision.

2. Common measures. A team leader aligns the team to a set of measures that clearly define what success looks like—setting in motion a sense of urgency, accountability and evaluation.

3. Efficient practices. A team leader guides the team to develop the plan and operate with practices and processes to deliver the objectives.

4. Defined roles. A team leader builds and maintains a team with the right talent, clear in their roles and responsibilities.

5. Sharp insights. A team leader creates an environment where teams gather data, create insights and continue learning.

6. Relevant rewards. A team leader focuses and motivates the team with the appropriate balance of rewards, recognition and celebration.

7. Consistent communication. A team leader makes certain that all team members' voices are heard and that formal and informal lines of communication remain open.

8. Solid culture. A team leader builds community based on trust, transparency and shared values.

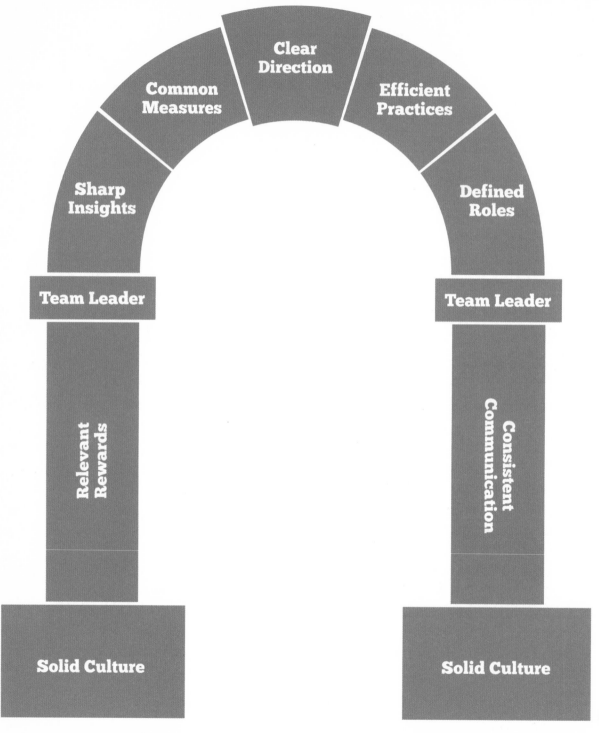

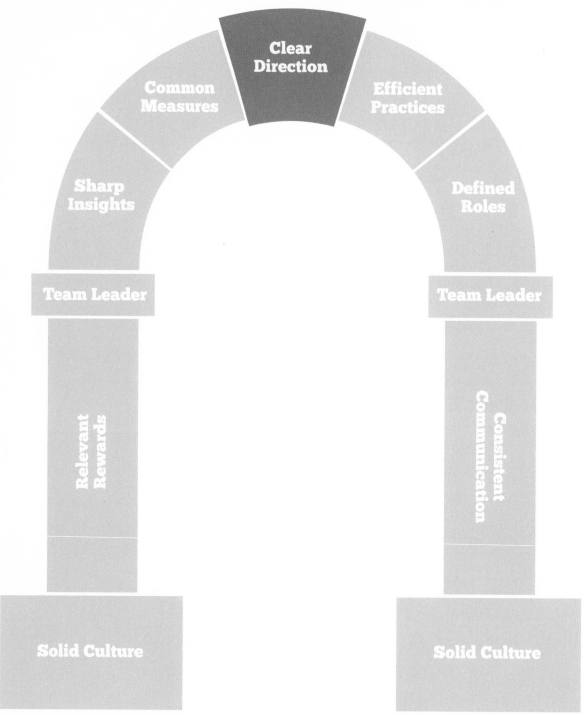

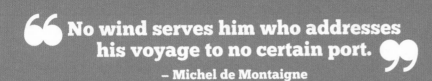

> **"No wind serves him who addresses his voyage to no certain port."**
> — Michel de Montaigne

Clear Direction

Way back in 1492, Christopher Columbus left Spain with a certain destination in mind. He had planned for it. He had recruited the right crew to help him get there. He had the backing and resources he needed. Christopher Columbus was headed for Asia.

Of course, there was that detail of traveling a path few, if any, had traveled before.

On several occasions, he had to reassess and revise his priorities. Barely a month into his voyage, Columbus and his crew made an extended stop in the Canary Islands. They were there for more than five weeks repairing, refitting and restocking the ships.

Columbus was not to be deterred. He was a man on a mission.

A mission that failed.

Or at least it would seem at first blush.

Though he never reached Asia, he did land upon a rather significant destination—one he wouldn't have reached had he simply set out for a long sail. He was prepared. He was focused. He was driven—like any successful team leader should be. While his destination was clear

> ## 66 You cannot change your destination overnight, but you can change your direction overnight. 99
> – Jim Rohn

and he had done what he could to prepare for the work required to reach his objective and goal, he did not end up where he thought he would. However, his mission was anything but a failure. Because his team was prepared, focused, determined and driven, Christopher Columbus actually found something better.

Like Columbus and his crew, a successful team recognizes and anticipates shifts in the wind. These teams consistently review and revise priorities based on results. Effective teams see that occasionally taking the clear course toward the original, clear direction leads the group to an unanticipated place. A new world perhaps.

Sometimes having a clear direction can take a team to places they—or anyone else—never dreamed. And other times, unlike Columbus, a clear direction gets you exactly where you intended.

3.2 Building a team bite by bite

Of all the elements of the Team Arch®, Clear Direction relies most heavily on team leadership. Someone must take the helm.

Sometimes a team is handed a mission. And sometimes, a team leader has the luxury of creating a team around a specific mission. In other instances, an existing team's mission may shift—and a leader is tasked with figuring out how to get from Point A to new Point B (think *Bad News Bears*).

Either way, some assembly is required.

The team should analyze the problem and determine the best means to eat the elephant bite-by-bite with the capabilities at hand—or decide when it's necessary to add or change players.

The team's capabilities are key. The collective intelligence (the team is capable of coming to a more complete and comprehensive solution because of each other) of a team, whether created to accomplish a short-term goal or to last for the long haul, should be able to sort through available data, possibilities and trajectory and make clear what is not.

Team members should be capable of gathering additional data, validating assumptions and generally challenging the thinking of the organization. Teams take

> ## 66 Of all the things I've done, the most vital is coordinating those who work with me and aiming their efforts at a certain goal. 99
> ### – Walt Disney

time and work best when the players are motivated and committed to one another—it's a bond that's tough to create, but possible to achieve when effectively using the Team Arch®. Clearly, people's personalities aren't going to change, but putting the pieces and processes together will create a team that is able to work toward a clear direction and lean on each other as needed.

In order to function as a cohesive unit, players should clock some time working together in the onset to achieve the goals—especially if the team is new. Without enough time in the saddle together and the chance to build a certain level of intimacy and trust, no one will know if these players can realistically achieve these objectives and goals.

The issue of time tends to be situational and goal-related. Collective intelligence, synergy and the team's ability to anticipate each other's actions will create something that is exceptional rather than acceptable—and takes time to create.

Some teams are simply required to get from Point A to Point B as fast as possible, and collective intelligence isn't necessary. If 'acceptable' will do for a given project, then the team can move quickly because a high level of synergy isn't required.

If the direction the team is headed or the goal requires more effort, then time must be taken. The team needs to gel from the beginning and when new members join the effort. Doing so acts as a safeguard against potential lapses in overall chemistry and synergy.

Some teams take time to hit their stride—and some never will.

> **66 Action to be effective must be directed to early conceived ends. 99**
>
> – Jawaharlal Nehru

3.3 How do you get there?
OGSM: Objectives, goals, strategies and measures

Whether a team is setting off to discover a new route, a new product or tackle a new sales goal, the first critical component is that all team members understand the group's objectives and goals. Without that alignment, the team will get nowhere fast. With it and when everyone on board has a clear understanding of the destination, getting there is easier.

The purpose of the Clear Direction component of the Team Arch® is to set direction. Focused priorities drive alignment on a team. Without this work, a team will never achieve its full potential.

In rare circumstances, teams automatically understand and are aligned to a definite and clear direction. However, even when teams know exactly where they want to go, they still have to form a cohesive approach in which route to take. Through the years, various businesses, sports teams and organizations have used hundreds, perhaps thousands, of methodical plans to set direction and determine their course to get there. One of the best and most efficient ways of delineating a team's clear direction and subsequent plans is a means called OGSM.

OGSM is a model that focuses on objectives, goals, strategies and measures and can work for almost any team or organization. It was developed in the '50s and '60s to align the direction of multinational corporations around the globe. The tool has since been adopted by many Fortune 500 companies.

The OGSM process requires rolling-up-your-sleeves and getting down to work. The team has to do the work together—and the work is not for the faint of heart. Going through the OGSM process requires the team to look at its performance through a critical and honest lens. The team must be candid about the work to do, the work that's been done and how

Why OGSM?

OGSM can be a powerful tool because it uses words and numbers to answer two key questions—what and how. OGSM harmonizes and aligns the team to what it needs to achieve—objectives and goals. OGSM transforms the objectives and goals into actionable and executable plans that clarify how to get there—strategies and measures. The process of creating an OGSM allows a team to:

- **Clearly define** its objectives (where it's going) and its goals (financial performance).
- **Crystallize** key strategies and initiatives.
- **Assign** owners and due dates.
- **Build** a one-page living document that can be the roadmap for all future planning reviews.

What do we need to achieve?		How do we get there?	
OBJECTIVES	**GOALS**	**STRATEGIES**	**MEASURES**
What we need to achieve:	What we need to achieve:	The choices we will make to achieve our objectives and goals, including key initiatives.	Numerical statements benchmarking progress toward implementing each strategy.
Objective statement	Financial and operational performance measures		
WORDS	**NUMBERS**	**WORDS**	**NUMBERS**

3.5
BUILDING AN OGSM

STEP 1
Outside-In assessment
- Roots the process in the internal and external realities
- Results in an honest discussion about the team

STEP 2
Affirm the company's objectives
- Creates a clear understanding of the target
- Produces an achievable vision for the team, which inspires and motivates

STEP 3
Solidify the current financial outlook
- Aligns the organization around growth expectations
- Grounds the process in financial realities

STEP 4
Create strategy platforms and initiatives
- Organizes the work around three key areas: growth, productivity and people
- Recognizes team strongholds, gaps and growth opportunities

STEP 5
Prioritize and resource the work
- Selects criteria to set priorities and allocate resources
- Identifies and groups the issues for resolution

STEP 6
Finalize the OGSM
- Converts the work into a living tool
- Launches the strategy into the team

STEP 7
Align and cascade the team
- Links team goals to divisional/functional goals and ultimately to the individual
- Culminates in a coordinated, measurable movement toward common business objectives and strategies

STEP 8
Implement management routine
- Ensures the OGSM lives in the team on a daily basis
- Communicates, reinforces and tracks execution

> 66 **On this team, we're all united in a common goal: to keep my job.** 99
> – Lou Holtz

to move forward. Many of the best teams have learned that an outside facilitator or person not involved in the work every day helps navigate the team through the OGSM process, avoiding landmines and pushing through to common ground.

The simplicity and beauty of the OGSM model is that the process requires teams to create a one-page working document that acts as a strategic/tactical roadmap.

The OGSM framework forms the basis for strategic planning and execution as well as subsequent reviews. It brings visibility and accountability to the core objectives of the organization and ensures activities are aligned to the financial goals. Due to the concise one-page format, it allows for quick management routine of any initiatives that are off target. And finally, it works because it is simple, robust, flexible and developed as a team.

3.6 Going deeper: building action plans to support the OGSM

Some of the strategies created during the OGSM process may have more moving parts than others and may require an action plan to ensure execution. An action plan identifies each of the steps required to deliver the project in more detail. Made up of many tasks, it delineates the steps necessary to accomplish a specific element of the strategy.

A team that creates successful action plans starts with the strategy and works backwards to clarify the work needed to drive execution.

The action plan's owner plays a critical role in a successful outcome. Even if he or she is minimally involved in getting the work done, having that person manage the process and consistently remind other team members what they need to do to get the job done is vital. The owner has the necessary task of making sure the plan is on track. Sometimes these projects are so long-term and large that it's easy to get distracted. For many action plan owners, a daily visual reminder helps to stay the course.

3.7
STEPS TO CREATE A SUCCESSFUL ACTION PLAN

1. The team or the team leader designates the right person to "own" the action plan and identifies the players needed for the team.

2. Start the action plan discussion with the end in mind.

3. Gather the players and have a brainstorming session to consider all the moving parts between where the team is and its target.

4. Delineate and sequence benchmarks by connecting specific dates to specific tasks. Understand interdependency of tasks. Deadlines are crucial to productivity; one task could be dependent on another phase's completion.

5. Create a working document sharing the entire action plan and align key stakeholders.

6. Post and monitor the action plan, sending out regular (preferably weekly) updates and reminders. Evaluate team members. Recalibrate and reconsider tasks required.

> ## 66 It takes little talent to see what lies under one's nose, a good deal to know in what direction to point that organ. 99
> – W. H. Auden

3.8 Pushing against a goal

Of all the elements of the Team Arch®, Clear Direction relies most heavily on team leadership. Someone must take the helm. Once a team knows and embraces its direction and a working rhythm is reached, an experienced team leader will be able to determine if the team's objectives and goals are realistic given the existing players—a skill that is part art and part science.

A strong team leader must be able to evaluate multiple pressures to determine if the team's goals are achievable and, eventually, to navigate a path toward success. The leader must be able to consider the market forces pressing against the goal, the competition and market trends. Simultaneously, the leader must weigh any other external forces.

3.9 Determining a team's capacity

Once a leader has a grasp of the external pieces of the puzzle, he or she processes the internal factors to determine the capability, tenure and experience of the team—the team's capacity.

Part of the leader's skill set is learned by reading the team, which is, in essence, reading people. Reading people accurately is an insight that can be honed by working with many people and paying close attention to recognize and associate character traits, strengths and weaknesses. A rare few have this gift innately, but the truth is that many who believe they do, in fact, do not.

Long-time leaders sometimes fall into a recurring, lethal trap in which they are constantly told only what they want to hear—actions that, over time, dilute a leader's "people-reading" skill set. Such is the problem with power.

Teams don't work to their full potential if a leader accepts or encourages all, some or a few players who consistently only say what the leader wants to hear. Real leaders appreciate team players who have the courage to say, "The emperor is wearing no clothes"—a trait that is oft rewarded in movies but not in the boardroom.

However, without that honesty, the team will never reach its true potential and will likely stagnate and even collapse.

The bad news is that there is no "just add water" technique in learning how to read people. The good news is that for those not born with this innate gift, it is a skill that can be strengthened by a few key behaviors.

NOTES:

Tips on reading people and making teams work

A rare few are born with an innate ability to read others. The rest of us can learn from hints and clues, making the most of key pointers to better understand people around us.

The most important reminder is that people who are adept at reading others naturally and consistently remember to first try to understand, then to be understood. In this pursuit of understanding, good people readers take into account a variety of factors including body language, facial expressions, vocal tone and word choice.

People, who are innately good at reading others, and those who want to become better, also look at environmental clues. They notice desk accessories, the style of car, if a car is messy or neat, jewelry, makeup, piercings/tattoos, etc. If they are able to visit someone's home, they realize the depth of understanding someone's home automatically offers about its residents.

Whatever the clue, good people readers automatically ask, "What does this tell me about a person?" People who are good at reading other people do not make snap judgments. They do not jump to the nearest conclusion and run with it. They continue to gather information and look for patterns. Recognizing behavioral patterns is key to understanding others—and recognizing patterns takes some time.

Therefore, people who are particularly good at reading others are patient. They do not seek to characterize the people around them and put them in labeled boxes. They seek understanding. They want to know, "What makes this person tick?"

Once a pattern has been established, good people readers begin to look for discrepancies. Discrepancies in the pattern tell a lot. For example, does the affable junior executive have a tendency to be rude to waiters? Good people readers have paid enough attention to others to figure out what the discrepancies mean.

One of the keys to reading people is to be as objective as possible. Try as we may, being completely objective is simply impossible. However, being aware of our biases, prejudices and projections goes a long way toward establishing a more objective frame of mind. This allows us to detect the strengths in those whom we might naturally reject and weaknesses in those who charm us past good logic.

People who read others well are naturally curious and tend to be skilled at asking questions—not in a nosy or accusatory way, but rather by gently delving deeper and getting to know someone better. They understand the types of questions necessary to help confirm or contradict assumptions made based on observation.

While reading people is largely based on observational skills and curiosity, intuition also plays an important role. A good leader generally has strong intuitions and has paid enough attention to his or her own patterns of success and failure, especially as those highs and lows relate to intuition. The bottom line: In reading people, a good leader knows when it's important to listen to intuition even when the data gathered says otherwise.

> 66 **Many are stubborn in pursuit of the path they have chosen, few in pursuit of the goal.** 99
> – Friedrich Nietzsche

3.11
CONSISTENTLY REVIEW AND REVISE PRIORITIES

Once a team has defined its OGSM and built required action plans, it is on its way toward clear direction.

Team members and the team leader must regularly review the organization's priorities relative to internal and external factors. Once on the correct trajectory, prioritization is easier and has fewer barriers. The challenge is to stay on track and adhere to the action plan alongside the bombardment of the day—customers, shipping, equipment and other variables that must be addressed.

3.12
Meaningful direction

People have to see it and feel it before they can change it, according to John P. Kotter, author of *The Heart of Change*. If a team's clear direction doesn't carry great weight, peak results will never be reached. In short, a team's objectives and goal have to be meaningful.

In post-Katrina Louisiana, the gravity of the New Orleans Saints' near-perfect 2009-2010 season extended well beyond what most football fans saw on the surface—a professional football franchise with a winning record.

No one recognized what a winning team meant for New Orleans more than quarterback Drew Brees and Coach Sean Payton. Both have often spoken of the need for hope and optimism in a region devastated by the greatest natural disaster the United States has ever known. Six months after Katrina, Payton was doing his best to recruit Brees, who was recuperating from surgery to repair a shoulder injury—an injury many believed would end his football career.

"This was the only team that really looked at me and said, 'We trust you.

We have confidence in you. We believe in you,'" Brees said. "Sometimes that's all you need is for somebody to believe in you and accomplish what you thought you could." Even still, the Miami Dolphins were interested in signing Brees to lead their team.

When Brees and his wife were visiting New Orleans on the recruiting trip, Payton decided to drive them on a tour around town to show how far the city had come in rebuilding. Instead, the coach got lost, taking an unintentional detour to an area completely obliterated by Katrina and her aftermath. It was the worst of the worst—with no sign of rebuilding or clean up.

Payton thought he had blown the whole deal. "And I thought to myself, 'I might as well drive them right to Miami. We have no shot at signing him,'" Payton said.

But for Brees and his wife, the sight of street after street of destruction had a different effect. "What most people might see as devastation and, 'I want no part of this,' we saw as a challenge," Brees said. Both he and his wife have said they felt a calling to the city.

For die-hard and new-to-the-game Saints fans, the complete 2009-2010 season was magical. New Orleans Saints fans began to call their quarterback Breesus. Many credited him with the resurrection of the city.

A winning football season gave many in and around New Orleans a positive focus. "It was so needed," Payton said. "The cars were going the other direction. They weren't coming in. And, here came hope."

By the time the Super Bowl finally arrived and the blessed Saints had made it, the streets, restaurants and bars of New Orleans and beyond were filled with people who simply could not stop smiling. The electricity was palpable. The positive momentum created by the team's success on the football field lifted the spirits of an entire region.

After a Herculean personal effort, and while still on the field with the New Orleans' Super Bowl dream finally realized, quarterback Brees stood with the NFC Championship trophy in hand and explained how his unlikely team was able to make their miracle season happen: "We just had to stay the course."**

* All quotes except the last one in this section are from 60 Minutes, originally aired on Sept. 26, 2010
** Fox NFL Sunday, Jan. 24, 2010

3.13 Watch Out!

Got resources? In order for a team to accomplish its goals, team members must have access to the basic resources it needed to get the job done. Without proper resources, teams will waste significant time and energy and lose momentum.

3.14 Steady the direction

A team leader can (and should) steady the direction of the team by:

- Maintaining focus on the long-term goals of the business.
- Learning to buffer the team from regular changes.
- Learning to anticipate the changes as they come from leadership or the marketplace.

Team leaders are like any leaders in that they can shield their people from the minutia that surrounds the daily operations of any business.

As the team considers the market conditions, needs of the business and desires of their customers, they have to respond appropriately. Priorities shift. The team constantly has to assess, adjust and revise the priorities. It is a constant balance between what is required and what is nice to have.

Team leaders have to know how much information to share with the team and prepare them for any major shifts. This is a steadying process—it protects morale, and anticipates shifts in strategy. Then the leader communicates clearly how those shifts will impact the direction of the team. Few things unbalance the team like receiving a whole new direction without warning or late in the game.

> ## **"Efforts are not enough without purpose and direction."**
>
> **– John F. Kennedy**

Summary
Chapter 3: Clear Direction

1. **Setting direction:** To create and maintain a clear direction, everyone on the team must understand the mission.

2. **Planning:** The team needs to have a clearly defined approach and action plan toward achieving the mission.

3. **Aligning:** Teams get aligned around the mission and the action required.

4. **Capabilities:** The team's goals must be reasonable with respect to the team's capabilities.

5. **Priorities:** The team has to know and embrace the top priorities.

6. **Resources:** The team must have the resources to get the job done.

7. **Measures:** While working together, the team needs to know how success is defined.

8. **Reflection:** The team should consistently review and revise priorities based on its performance.

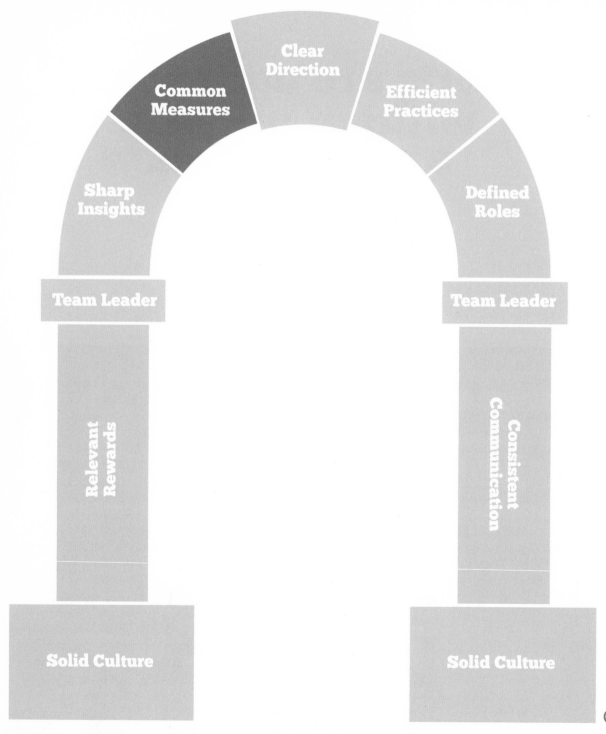

> **In God we trust, all others bring data.**
> – W. Edwards Deming

Common Measures

On a cold January night in 1934 in Dallas Center, Iowa, the high school basketball team was playing neighboring rival, Adel.

The back-and-forth game was coming down to the closing seconds. At that point in American sports, an official timekeeper, appointed by the home team, used a stopwatch to manage the game's time. The opposing team appointed a time-keeping monitor, who used a different stopwatch, to keep things honest.

When time was out, the official timekeeper would fire a starter gun to signal the end of the game.

In the middle of Iowa corn country on that cold night long ago, Adel had the ball when the official timekeeper fired the gun signaling the end of the game. Dallas Center, the home team, was ahead by two.

Just after the closing gun was fired, one of Adel's players launched a shot and made a basket. As the shot went in, the time monitor (appointed by the team who made the basket) began waving his stopwatch in the air, saying that the points should count. He believed the official timekeeper had ended the game seconds early.

"That was the point where my dad, who was Dallas Center's superintendent, kind of messed up," said 86-year-old Jacques Foster, who was a young boy at the time and had left the game early. "Dad could have said, very easily, 'Time was out. The game is over. We're turning out the lights.' And everybody would have just gone home."

But that's not what happened.

Instead Elmer E. Foster said, "These are our guests. We're going to count the basket. We're going to play an overtime. That's fair play."

Dallas Center ended up losing in overtime.

"The home team was next to violent," Jacques Foster said. "There was a crowd waiting outside for my dad. He left the gymnasium by the furnace room door."

On his trip home that night, Superintendent Foster made up his mind that there had to be a better way.

"He said on his way home, 'I'm going to build a big clock. It will keep the time and blow the horn. I'm going to call it Fair-Play,'" Jacques Foster said.

Superintendent Foster was also a science teacher and began working to figure out how to make his idea a reality. With the help of the local jeweler, Foster created a large clock with a horn. It worked well, and the fans loved it. He decided to patent his idea.

"Before long, other schools who played there wanted one too. Dad and some other teachers made scoreboards for them—getting reimbursed for the parts—but that quickly got out of hand," remembered Jacques Foster of his father's early timekeeping, horn-blowing contraptions.

By 1938, the demand for scoreboards had grown so much that the superintendent had to make a choice between the field of education or pursuing his burgeoning new business full-time.

The business' growth continued and went beyond simple scoreboards for high school gymnasiums. As audiences became more engaged in the games they were watching, Fair-Play's boards became more elaborate and sophisticated, and they began to add more and more bells and whistles (literally).

Four decades after Foster barely made it out of the high school gym, *Sports Illustrated* featured a photo of him and a story about the new Fair-Play scoreboard at Dodger Stadium. *Sports Illustrated* credited Foster's company with ushering in the modern message-board era. By that time, Jacques Foster was working with the company, as well. He remembers the Dodger's scoreboard but says the Astrodome's 1965 so-called "exploding scoreboard" was the pinnacle of the family's success in his mind. "It added a whole new dimension to sports," he said.

These days, squawking, talking, multicolored scoreboards are standard fare for most sports fans—in large thanks to Elmer E. Foster's desire for a better, more transparent way to engage the audience in the legitimacy of the process.

> **Ben Franklin may have discovered electricity— but it is the man who invented the meter who made the money.**
> — Earl Warren

Without scoreboards, coaches, teams and fans still would be reduced to unruly disputes on exactly when the timer went off. How often would a Solomon-like figure such as Elmer E. Foster step up to offer the opposing team another chance?

Instead, scoreboards put the information out there for everyone to see—how many goals or the number of points scored, how much time is left and the penalties or notable rewards gained along the way. The presence of the scoreboard also shows the gap between where a team stands and how many points it needs to win—and the time or scope to reach the goal.

Creating organizational scorecards does the same for a team in any business or organization. People know where they stand. They know what's expected of them. They know how much time they've got to make another goal.

Setting measureable goals and keeping clear, accurate data exposed for all to see is critical to making the Team Arch® work. It's fair play.

4.2 Creating a team scorecard

An effective scorecard focuses and guides a team. Plus, it aligns the team's efforts to the organization's goals. Unlike scoreboards, a team's scorecard doesn't require lots of bells and whistles. Team scorecards can be simple but must be structured and focused. Teams must document what they are trying to accomplish and communicate the goals correctly so the right expectations are set.

> ## 66 You get what you measure. Measure the wrong thing and you get the wrong behaviors. 99
> — John H. Lingle

An industrial manufacturing business in Brussels decided to mount a 10 x 20 foot scorecard on the wall. They completely dedicated themselves to tracking and managing revenue, expenses, transportation methods, on-time delivery, sales and profit—to create a rare level of transparency in the company. Like a scoreboard in a basketball game, team members could see the gap. It helped align the team, and the transparency gave visibility throughout the system.

Without clear posting of the performance of a business, it is difficult for team members to engage. In the case of the team in Brussels, their giant scorecard helped to create buy-in for each team member. A strong scorecard uses recurring metrics to establish wins for the team and issue alerts to problems. To keep the scorecard meaningful, a team should establish regular and periodic reviews of the scorecard. Just like the clock at a basketball game, the posted numbers added a sense of urgency to get the job done—and get it done on time.

Elmer E. Foster, the creator of the electronic scoreboard, often said hearing a crowd count down, "Ten, nine, eight, seven…" was music to his ears. Just think, before electronic scoreboards, such a countdown was impossible. The only people with a sense of exactly how much time were the two official timekeepers. That left the rest of the crowd—and even the players—in the dark.

Sharing measurements of performance gets the whole team involved. Increased transparency shifts ownership from the team leader to the team—making the team members openly accountable. Of all dynamics in the Team Arch®, the scorecard is where urgency is created on the team.

4.3 What should a scorecard score?

Detailed scorecards may feature references to company strategic goals including financial performance, customer-focused outcomes, talent management and market competition. However, the trick in creating an effective scorecard lies in knowing what to measure that is critical to your organization's success.

Attempting to measure too much is a common mistake in creating scorecards. For example, a team might attempt to measure a significant number of things that affect customer satisfaction. They could measure quality of service, speed of service, pricing, complaints, problem resolution or effectiveness of account management.

Measuring too much is cumbersome and unwieldy. However, measuring too little limits information or slows down corrective action. Scorecards need not be complex, but they do need to be specific, clear and accurate—and clarity and accuracy require team input.

In addition to the team's overall goals, a team scorecard sets the targets and measurements for each team member. There is a direct connection between the team scorecard and each team member's goals and responsibilities. This link gives each team member clear performance measures and creates transparency for everyone on the team.

CREATING AN EFFECTIVE SCORECARD

In creating an effective scorecard, the team has to identify the specific measures that will define success. Those measures must be based on four criteria that assess the team's effectiveness, directly or indirectly. The scorecard should:

- ■ Include measures that represent what the team is trying to accomplish.
- ■ Be accessible and possible to gather.
- ■ Be timely.
- ■ Offer a predictive toward the future.

4.4 Making the scorecard work

Many might believe the team leader best manages the scorecard. In fact, the team members are the best managers of a team scorecard. Everyone on the team takes ownership when it comes to delivering the measures. In addition, the purpose of the team scorecard is to get a true measure of how the team is doing as a whole. When the team views its performance from a number of perspectives, it gains a more accurate assessment that promotes "team-think" and allows every member to have a stake in the team's performance.

The scorecard should be a tool that brings the team together and focuses it, as opposed to simply becoming a reporting mechanism that the team reviews on a regular basis—whether it's every week or every other week. It should also be reviewed on a monthly and annual basis. The scorecard should not measure simply how many sales calls an employee has every day, but how much revenue is generated by each call. Forcing employees to focus on an arbitrary number of calls is just reporting, not focusing on the goal of the team. Requiring teams to come together to review the scorecard regularly provides a space for the team to self-regulate—which is the overall purpose of a scorecard.

4.5 Creating clear individual performance measures

In an effective scorecard, individual team members own elements of performance both individually and collectively. For example, the supply chain and manufacturing lead has a performance measure of lowering the cost of goods eight percent or the human resources team member might have employee retention as a measure on the scorecard.

Clearly delineated ownership of the elements of performance is critically important to team success. Clear ownership ensures that goals are met. And for those times when the team is not performing, ownership helps determine indicators of performance—or lack thereof.

As the elements are assigned, the team leader must work with the team to be certain members understand how the different pieces of the puzzle interrelate and how each piece is necessary for the overall success of the scorecard. In fact, many successful teams transfer and translate the measures to the individual level and create individual performance measures for each team member.

4.6
ROOT CAUSE ANALYSIS

Getting to the root cause of an issue is the crux of solving the problem. Looking at data at the wrong level can send anyone down the wrong path. For example, if a sales team misses a target, the natural instinct may be to conclude that the team needs to make more sales.

A closer look at the situation reveals that the team made more sales than the shipping center was able to fulfill. There simply wasn't enough product to ship because the system didn't have enough lead time built in to have products ready for orders. The root cause of the problem was an issue with forecasting. Addressing and fixing the snafu with forecasting would go a long way in allowing the sales team to meet their goal.

W. Edwards Deming's *5 Why's* concept provides a great place to start in identifying root cause. Simply ask five *Why* questions to uncover the root of the problem.

1. Why are sales off?

2. Why couldn't we fulfill the orders?

3. Why are we not shipping enough?

4. Why don't we have the appropriate inventory?

5. Why don't we have the right forecast?

4.7

TAKING THE SCORECARD A STEP FURTHER:
OPEN-BOOK MANAGEMENT

The concept of open-book management is simple. By opening the books and making management transparent to everyone on a team or company, employees do understand more about the workings of their company and do their jobs better.

This means extensive information sharing with all employees including, but not limited to, revenue, profit, cost of goods, cash flow and expenses.

According to John Case, who coined the term in 1993 and authored *Open Book Management: The Coming Business Revolution*, "Opening the books means a whole lot more than just announcing the quarterly results the way publicly traded companies do. It means communicating all the relevant information, monthly or weekly or daily, to people in every plant or department or store or unit within a company. No executive in his or her right mind would wait until the books are closed at the end of a quarter to gauge a unit's performance. And no employee who wants to act like a businessperson should have to make do with old data, either. …What we're talking about here, however, isn't just open books. It's open-book management."

In *The Great Game of Business*, author Jack Stack lays out three basic rules for open-book management:

1. Know and teach the rules:

Every employee should be given the measures of business success and taught to understand them.

2. Follow the action and keep score:

Every employee should be expected and enabled to use their knowledge to improve performance.

3. Provide a stake in the outcome:

Every employee should have a direct stake in the company's success—and in the risk of failure.

Critical Numbers:

Typically, open-book management focuses on a critical number to effect change. The number differs from company to company, but it represents a key gauge of profitability—a break-even point. With the critical number, companies develop a scorecard to track and indicate progress toward the critical number.

4.8
MEASURING IN BASEBALL

"Although they do not tell the entire story of baseball, they are more than endless columns of numbers. For if they only inspire the human aspect of the people they represent, they have achieved a sound purpose."

—*from the opening pages of The Sports Encyclopedia: Baseball by David S. Neft*

Way back in September 1965, the Los Angeles Dodgers were fighting the San Francisco Giants for a spot to play the Minnesota Twins in the World Series. Sandy Koufax was on the cover of *The Sporting News.* Deep in the pages of the publication, another baseball story was in the making. It was a quiet story that was a long time coming. In the bottom left-hand corner of page 20, there was a small ad.

That ad was placed by David S. Neft, who had been obsessed with numbers for most of his life. He played baseball as a kid, but by his own accord, his abilities were "not of consequence." However, he grew up in New York City within walking distance of two major league ballparks and watched the likes of Joe DiMaggio rack up his 56-game hitting streak, Ted Williams was the last player in the major leagues to bat over .400 in a single season and Willie Mays plowed through eight consecutive 100-RBI seasons.

In 1965, Neft founded Information Concepts, Inc. and led a group of researchers, some college students, to compile and create the first comprehensive computerized database of baseball statistics. Neft and his researchers scoured libraries

and old newspapers across the country to fill in the blanks of professional baseball and verify incomplete statistics, bringing to life the names and records of some previously unrecognized players.

Four years after beginning the massive undertaking, Macmillan Publishing printed 50,000 copies of *The Baseball Encyclopedia*, a seven-pound, 2,300-page definitive work of baseball statistics compiled by Neft and his team. Over the years, the book sold more than 100,000 copies, according to Neft.

Beyond gathering all of professional baseball's facts and figures, the epic project became a testing ground for computers' data storage and analytical abilities and is believed to be the first conventional book typeset entirely by computer in the country.

Neft is particularly proud that the work, certified by Major League Baseball, provided a new perspective on the old game. In fact, two players, Sam Thompson, an amazing RBI hitter, and Addie Joss, with the second best career earned run average in Major League history, were elected to the National Baseball Hall of Fame because of Neft's work.

"There are different levels and different uses of the stats, but the obvious value of the stats to players and owners—depending on whether the stats are good or bad—is in contract negotiations," Neft said.

According to Neft, teams use gathered statistics in evaluating the players and, in some cases, to determine strategy—wisdom easily transferred from the ballpark to the boardroom.

"'Who would you use in a certain situation? Whether you're going to intentionally walk somebody? Who you're going to use against a certain pitcher to pinch hit?' Things that aren't determined by statistics, but statistics make them more evident," he said.

What word of caution does Neft offer about statistics and the value of numbers in general? "Beware of small sample sizes," he said. After all, batting a thousand isn't a big deal if you're only up to bat one time.

Lesson for the team:

Understanding the measures can change the game. Sometimes simple tactical choices based on good measures can make all the difference.

4.9 Sense of urgency

Anyone who's ever heard a two-minute warning timer ring understands the urgency the time element of a scoreboard creates.

Teams get lulled into a false sense of success when scores don't get posted and reviewed openly. Without the score and the time, the sense of urgency is lost. Dynamically, the scope, time and gap to the goal work together to create a sense of urgency. The same factors work for the scorecard as well.

Without regular reminders, teams lose sight of road markers and often don't realize when they're headed in the wrong direction or when team members are working on the wrong things.

Creating a sense of urgency is important because it pushes a team to be nimble. If necessary, the team's members can call a metaphorical timeout and change the course of action midstream so that they can improve performance against the gap they're facing.

To use another sports analogy, in a hockey game when a team is down in the final stretch, they often take away the goalie and add a scorer to the ice. The risk is there by lowering the defense, but sometimes all hands on deck focused on offense is the only way to win. A team has to be able to shift gears and resources to try to drive toward the anticipated goal.

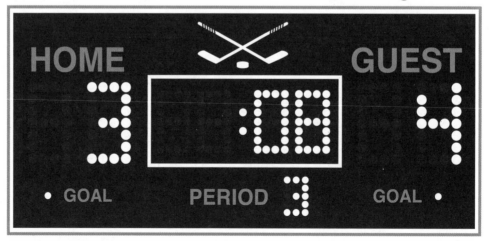

4.10 Watch Out:
Easy-to-track valid measures

In creating an effective scorecard, there are three pitfalls too many teams discover only after it's too late:

1. The team must be realistic about what it is measuring.

2. The team must understand it is required to collect the data.

3. The team must be certain to measure the right things.

Countless teams have created elaborate scorecards—works of beauty, really. The only problem was that the scorecards permanently retained their pristine beauty due to a complete lack of use.

A scorecard that isn't realistic about what it's measuring, or that requires data impossible to collect becomes meaningless. Few, if any, will fill out those scorecards if information a team just can't capture is required. Scorecards are not the place for aspirations. Scorecards must be realistic.

The flipside to unrealistic scorecards is those that measure the wrong things. In the 1990s, one of the world's largest consumer-package goods companies measured the success of its sales people by the number of calls representatives made each day. Representatives were smart enough to plan their days around corners with lots of smaller retail outlets where they often made mediocre sales but were rewarded handsomely for visiting plenty of stores—as opposed to focusing sufficient time on stores that could make a bigger impact on the business.

Additionally, there are qualitative measures that make considerable difference in how a team operates. The intangibles of the work a team does are essential but often more difficult to measure. Financials, of course, are easy. They've been defined—profitable or not profitable. It's more difficult to measure that a team member successfully mentored two peers, but the intangibles of business are important and detrimental when ignored. Finding the means to objectively measure these aspects of the work a team does is critical.

> ## **"Measure what is measurable, and make measurable what is not so."**
>
> **— Galileo Galilei**

Summary
Chapter 4: Common Measures

1. **Defining measures:** The team has a scorecard that tracks performance.

2. **Transparency:** The team's scorecard is visible to all.

3. **Accountability:** Team members have clear individual performance measures.

4. **Ease:** A team's measures are easy to track and validate.

5. **Timeliness:** The team's scorecard is monitored regularly—weekly, monthly and annually.

6. **Management routine:** The team has a regular review of the scorecard and based on progress, adjustments are made to the plan.

7. **Self-regulation:** Everyone on the team takes ownership when it comes to reviewing and delivering the measures.

8. **Urgency:** The scorecard instills a sense of urgency for the team.

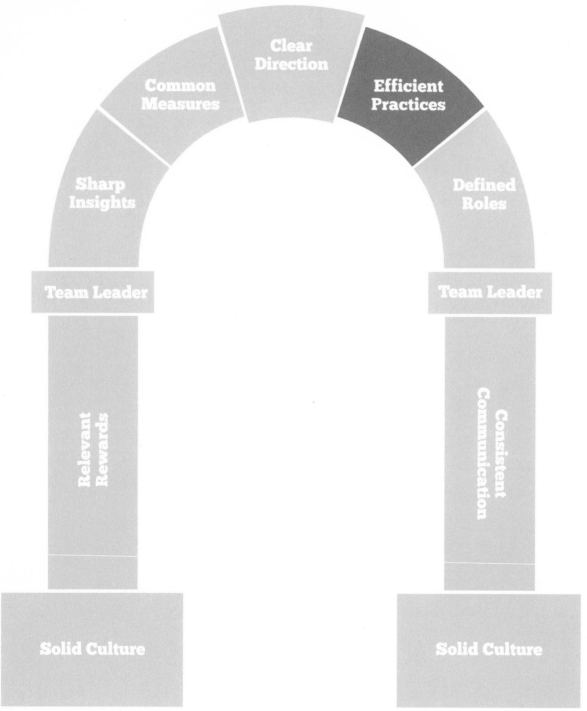

5

Efficient Practices

Of the nearly 20,000 acres of parks and gardens inside the 26 miles of walls around Versailles, King Louis XIV was most obsessed with the chateau's spectacular fountains.

Yes, fountains. And lots of them. During parts of his reign between 1643 and 1715, Louis XIV seemed determined to conquer nature for his own vanity and amusement. The trouble was Versailles didn't have a water source. The quantity and pressure of its water supply simply was insufficient for the Sun King's grandiose visions.

Using elaborate engineering efforts requiring thousands of laborers and vast quantities of money, Louis XIV went to extreme efforts to bring as much water as possible to Versailles. In 1684, his most complex building scheme, La Machine de Marly, began diverting and pushing water uphill from the Seine to Versailles.

With this new water source in place, the royal palace began using as much water as the entire city of Paris. But even that wasn't enough. To satiate his never-ending thirst, the king demanded newer contraptions and additional channels to divert even more water into Versailles. Yet, there was never enough water to simultaneously operate all 2,400 of Versailles' fountains.

> ## 66 The efficient man is the man who thinks for himself. 99
> — Charles William Elliot

Be that as it may, Louis insisted on seeing all fountains operating.

So, his team of gardeners and engineers devised a plan. They stationed boys with whistles throughout the gardens to signal which fountains should run based on the king's location. Using simple ingenuity, they made sure Louis XIV and his royal guests, when walking about the gardens, saw fully functional fountains at all times.

Granted, at Louis' command, his engineers developed an efficient system to keep the king happy, but as Peter Drucker said, "Nothing is less productive than to make more efficient what should not be done at all."

5.2 The difference between efficient and effective

To Drucker's point, the difference between efficiency and effectiveness is the difference between doing things right and doing the right things.

Once a team is clear on its direction, creating efficient practices is fundamental to the Team Arch®. Common team practices include meetings, conflict resolution, team planning, problem solving, communications and hand-offs between departments or team members. Most team practices are defined and made up of sequential steps called work processes.

A work process is a series of definable, repeatable and predictable work activities, which together produce the results required to please an internal or external customer. Work processes are not sexy, but they're required.

Many team processes are interrelated. A breakdown in one could lead to a breakdown in another, resulting in confusion and contributing to conflict. This combination may cause a team to lose focus, momentum and overall achievement. Improving a team practice requires a disciplined dismantling of the status quo to establish more efficient practices. Again, the work isn't easy but it is required.

The most efficient and effective teams have a standard way of getting things done. They have discipline. They work in processes, and those processes increase productivity. Left unattended, workflow morphs like a river taking the path of least resistance. It creates divergent streams and spreads to people who get the work done. The result is that those who do more, get more to do and those who do less are left without work.

5.3 Making processes better

To correct inefficiencies, work processes must be improved, but first the processes must be standardized.

Many teams work using customization versus standardization. Customized workflows create high levels of inefficiency with haphazard zigging and zagging of work going from person to person and place to place. These customized workflows are often highly evolved and transferred from one employee to the next. What's usually missing, however, is someone who understands the haphazard method of getting work done who has the capacity and authority to ask why—as in, *"Why is this the accepted practice?"* and *"Why are we doing things this way?"*

Independent—rather than interdependent—workflow situations rarely produce top results.

It's the old, "I cut off the corner of the ham because my mother taught me to do so." (And the mother did it because her mother did.) Finally, someone asks Grandma, "Why do we cut off the corner of the ham?" Grandma replies, "I don't know." Mother says, "I do it because you did." Grandma laughs and says, "Oh, I remember now. I used to cut off the corner of hams so they would fit in the only pan that would fit inside my small oven."

> 66 **The first rule of any technology used in a business is that automation applied to an efficient operation will magnify the efficiency. The second is that automation applied to an inefficient operation will magnify the inefficiency.** 99
> — Bill Gates

Many teams often inherit "cut-off-the-corner-of-the-ham" work processes.

Customized—rather than standardized—practices that fit the current environment create a high level of confusion for team members.

The process needs to be considered, streamlined and made efficient. In order to create a more efficient standardized process, the old way of getting the task accomplished must first be defined. For many, the easiest way to define a process is to map it. Here's what a customized, inefficient process looks like before being standardized and improved.

Non-Standardized Process

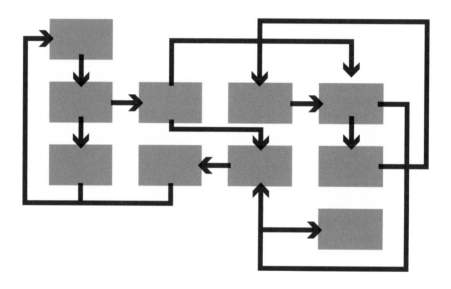

5.4 Standardized and non-standardized processes

In order to get to a better, more efficient way of operating, a team must standardize its processes so that each gets done the same way every time. To be clear, this is not an endorsement for a team to strive for robothood. However, standardizing key work practices, such as how a team does annual planning or how a meeting is conducted, cleans up slapdash messes that teams encounter.

Secondly, teams should take a close look at the desired outcome and improve the process by making it faster, cheaper, simpler or better aligned with customer requirements and expectations. When the process cannot be further improved, put the new solution in place.

However, once the new solution is in place, teams should not rest on their laurels. They should innovate. Innovation is about continuously improving. At least once a year, a team needs to evaluate its process for inefficiency and make adjustments to improve performance.

What follows is a diagram of a standardized and improved process. Note the savings the standardized process offers in time, steps and rework. This savings in turn will lead to improved reliability and internal and external customer satisfaction.

Standardized & Improved Process

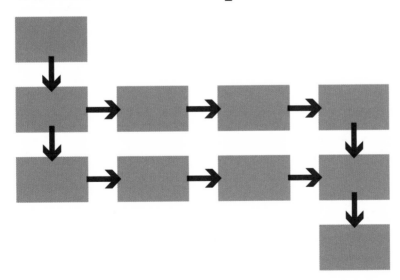

TRAITS OF EFFICIENT TEAMS

Way back in the infancy of stock car racing in 1950, the Wood Brothers Racing Team was formed on the Wood family farm in Virginia's Blue Ridge Mountains. The family's four sons had a talent for auto mechanics and spent much of their time at their father's garage. The Wood boys simply liked fixing and tinkering with cars.

With early success on the track, the Wood Brothers Racing Team turned the weekend hobby of Glen and Leonard into a full-time business. The other brothers, meanwhile, worked regular jobs and moonlighted with racing.

In the early days of motor racing, when a car needed service during a race, the driver would pull into the pits and turn the car off. Even back then, the off-track time couldn't be described as leisurely, but drivers would then get out of their cars and even smoke a cigarette as the crew took the necessary time to use a hand pump jack to change tires, fill the tanks and adjust or tend to what needed attention.

The Wood Brothers realized if they reduced the time during these stops, they could increase their time and position in the race on the track. The brothers began to work to limit the time during these stops by implementing specific processes and are credited with inventing what is now known as the pit stop.

As other teams noticed that the Wood Brothers were winning races due to their efficient pit stops, these competitors soon copied the Wood method. The Wood team practiced and perfected the pit stop to mimic an acrobatic, mechanical dance.

Glen Wood credits his brother Leonard's engineering skills with providing the necessary foundation for the innovation and for improving the equipment used by the team. Leonard Wood worked with Ingersoll-Rand to assist in developing pneumatic air-guns to wrench lug nuts off cars at super-sonic speeds. Leonard Wood took the

pneumatic idea a step further and developed the pneumatic jack. Between Leonard's improvements and innovations to the equipment and the lean and precise choreography of the actual pit stop, the Wood brothers brought the total time needed at the stop to exactly 20 seconds.

In 1965, the Wood Brothers were hired to run the pit for Jimmy Clark for the mother of all races—the Indianapolis 500. Clark won simply because he was in and out of the pits faster than anyone else in the race.

In recent years, as the sport has boomed in popularity and turned into a multi-billion dollar industry, former professional athletes, from the hockey rink to the football field, vie for positions on NASCAR seven-man pit crews and the $100,000-plus salaries that go with them.

Their athleticism, along with continued improvements in equipment and choreography has the pit crew changing four tires, filling the gas tank and making other adjustments in 14 seconds or less.

5.6
TEAM PROCESSES

Generally, most teams work in processes that can be broken up into eight areas:

1. Meeting management
2. Communication
3. Planning
4. Prioritization
5. Resource allocation
6. Problem-solving
7. Hand-offs and transitions
8. Conflict resolution

NOTES:

5.7

ASSESSING PROCESSES ON YOUR TEAM

How are you doing? Score your team on a scale from 1 ("Our team finds this very challenging")
to 5 ("This comes easily to our team, and we actively practice this regularly").

1 2 3 4 5   Our team has an effective approach to planning.

1 2 3 4 5   Our team has an effective approach to prioritizing work.

1 2 3 4 5   Our team has an effective approach to resource allocation.

1 2 3 4 5   Our team members consider our meetings
both effective and efficient.

1 2 3 4 5   In terms of problem-solving, our team is successful
and perpetually moves the organization forward.

1 2 3 4 5   Key work practices and processes are well defined
and followed by the team.

1 2 3 4 5   Hand-offs between team members are clear and
well managed.

1 2 3 4 5   Our team has an effective process to handle conflicts.

1 2 3 4 5   Our team regularly reviews and consistently improves
business practices.

> ❝The ultimate goal of a more effective and efficient life is to provide you with enough time to enjoy some of it.❞
> – Michael LeBoeuf

5.8 Don't forget about administrative and management processes

Over time, good manufacturers have used work process design to clean up their production facilities and make them incredibly efficient. However, the same organizations rarely carry over the same discipline to their administrative, sales, marketing, finance and management systems.

Manufacturing processes historically are characterized by considerably less waste and rework than most supporting processes. Consequently, better administrative processes offer a huge opportunity for reduced waste and improved quality.

The discipline of process control could also explain why manufacturing productivity has increased faster than administrative and management productivity.

Good management teams look for efficiency improvement in their work process regardless whether it's management, manufacturing or customer relations.

Discipline

Simply put, being a part of a successful team requires work discipline. All team members have to work efficiently to deliver their accountabilities across the board. Of course, processes get messy from time to time, but a culture of efficiency and accountability is essential to a successful team.

5.9 Going deeper–problem solving

As Groucho Marx said, "The easiest way to deal with problems is to not address them."

One of the biggest challenges for teams is solving difficult problems that spark up on the team. The crux of the matter is that difficult problems, for teams and individuals, usually have four common components:

- A lack of clarity of the situation
- A misalignment of multiple goals
- A large number of items, interrelations and decisions
- A definite, and often urgent, time consideration

Resolving a problem requires a team to work together to define and subsequently organize a direct attack on each of the four components of the problem.

5.10 Meeting management

While every team has its own unique set of issues and complications, the lowest hanging fruit for most teams interested in improving their processes are universal: meeting management and hand-offs between team members. Improving meetings can lead to significant improvements in overall performance.

Much of the root of the excessive meeting culture that the modern business world has created lies in low trust. "If I'm not invited to that meeting, will something happen that will adversely affect me?" Attending meetings becomes as much about CYA (cover your a**) as it is about the natural desire to be included.

Anything that is a result of low trust is bound to have difficulties. Most teams just don't do meetings well. Meetings, important as they are, have become inconsistent and inefficient. The time wasted in meetings is one of the chief complaints in corporate America. Part of the issue is having the discipline to slow down long enough to prepare appropriately for a meeting.

Making meetings more efficient increases speed, alignment and results. Plus, communication is clearer. The best meetings are meetings that center on decision-making—

SIX STEPS TO SOLVING A PROBLEM

1. Define the problem.

2. Identify the current approach or way of work that is creating the problem.

3. Describe all of the possible causes of the problem and agree on the root cause(s).

4. Prioritize the root causes.

5. Test possible solutions to determine best course of action.

6. Standardize the solution that works best for all parties involved.

not information sharing. When an organization brings 50 people into a room when they only need five, the chance of having a real discussion is almost impossible—productivity and efficiency are both decreased or even lost altogether.

When pulling people together, consider the economic value of having each person in the room. People who come to meetings should come prepared and informed on the situation that has led to the meeting.

If a meeting is about sharing information, send out the information in advance and use the meeting time for clarification, questions and discussions that lead to a decision and the next steps to be taken. The team's collective intelligence should improve the quality of the information, assessing risks and subsequent decisions.

Many times meetings are driven by culture rather than a need to get things done. As an example, a collaborative culture will tend to have more people at meetings than necessary. The reason is the value of having everyone's voice heard. The opposite is true in a command-and-control culture, where few people are pulled into the decision-making and meetings are more directive than empowering.

The bottom line is that regardless of culture, teams must develop meeting practices that conform to their culture while still effectively driving efficiency and performance.

MEETINGS IN A NUTSHELL

Once it is determined that a meeting is necessary, there are a number of helpful models to use to plan, structure and organize meetings. In a nutshell, teams can use the following key elements in preparing for meetings. Chances are teams know these. The question is: Do they do them regularly?

1. Participation

Who needs to be here? Attendance is based on people's responsibility for the key solutions to be discussed.

_____

_____

2. Agenda

How will we work through the meeting? What do I need to prepare for it? Each attendee receives a solid agenda with pre-work required.

_____

_____

3. Purpose

What are we here for? Participants should have a clear description of what the topic and deliverables are for the meeting.

_____

_____

4. Actions/Decisions

What actions and decisions are required? Attendees use a template for capturing action items and follow-up with people assigned to complete them.

_____

_____

5. Protocol

Are we safe and respectful? Good meetings begin and end on time and are conducted with participants' safety in mind—both in a physical sense and a psychological sense. No detail involving safety is too mundane or minor. The team should set meeting ground rules. For example:

- No cell phones.
- Start and end on time.
- Be respectful—listen to each other.
- Keep action items and follow up for next steps well defined.

_____

5.12 Assess your most recent meeting

1. How many people were needed in the meeting to make the decisions?

2. How many additional people were there?

3. Go ahead, calculate the number of wasted man hours the meeting took cumulatively.

4. Did the meeting require advance work to move the topics along?

5. Based on your observations, what percent of the advance work did attendees complete before the meeting began?

6. Did the meeting have an agenda?

7. Did the meeting follow the agenda?

8. Was the meeting centered on decision-making?

9. What percentage of the meeting was for information sharing?

10. Did the meeting have a clear purpose?

11. Did the meeting achieve its clear purpose?

12. Did the meeting start on time and end on time?

5.13 Hand-offs

If hand-offs don't happen, a group of people is not a team. Errors and delays most often occur at the margins on hand-off points between team members, departments or functional areas. Employees don't always understand the total process because often they don't know what happens after work leaves their desk.

The literal hand-off in a relay race is a great analogy for internal team hand-offs. Anyone who has ever watched a relay race recognizes that the beauty of winning as a team is in the hand-off. Members of the relay team have to anticipate one another. They have to have a process to exchange the baton, and timing is everything.

The best relay racers do not look at one another when exchanging the baton. The reason is simple. It's faster to keep looking ahead. Those hand-offs work because the runners are members of a well-oiled machine. They know exactly what the process is—where to be and when to be there. Likewise, a botched hand-off can seriously derail a team.

A swim relay medley race is another good comparison for a team solving a problem. To win the race, the strongest swimmer for each stroke competes—similar to teammates with different strengths working together to complete a task with successful hand-offs.

5.14
Pitfalls of team hand-offs

COMING IN TOO FAST
One team member expects another team member to be ready to receive data or a deliverable and the second team member is not in position to move forward.

COMING IN TOO SLOW
One team member is not expecting another to be ready, when, in fact, the second team member has been waiting around.

MISSING THE HAND-OFF
A team member misses a critical deadline and throws the timing off, killing productivity.

DROPPING THE BATON
A team member fails to deliver as requested—or at all.

5.15 Making email more effective and efficient

Email changed much of the face of the modern work style. Its immediacy and convenience led to what many initially believed was communication nirvana. And then, it took over. Making email work rather than letting it control a day and seep into all phases of life requires diligence.

When you're the sender:

1. Make sure email is the right way to communicate the message. Sending an email message is one-way communication. A conversation, in person or over the phone guarantees an immediate response. Email does not. Sometimes email even takes more time than a conversation. Additionally, email doesn't easily convey nonlinear thoughts. If you need an immediate response, anticipate follow-up questions or need to convey a complex topic using charts and graphs, email is probably not the way to go.

2. Get to the point immediately. Ask your questions. Provide your answer within the first few sentences of your message. Wait until later to give details and explanations.
   Good: Hey, could you send me a copy of the ad you created for AIO? I need it for my presentation this afternoon.
   Bad: Hey, I checked my inbox and my voicemail and noticed I hadn't received the copy of the AIO ad yet. I should have had it last Monday because the meeting I'm going to this afternoon is really important. Have you finished it yet? If so, I'd like to see it.

3. If you have a question, be certain to ask the question. Don't assume the receiver understands your statement and will respond with the information you need.

4. Be clear about who should respond.

5. Be clear about when you need a response.

6. Limit the number of topics in each message.

7. No matter how hip or cool you see yourself, use proper grammar and punctuation.

8. Provide enough context so that people who don't have the topic top-of-mind will understand the situation or question.

Good: Thanks for taking the time to chat with me yesterday after the meeting about your decision not to go to the GAU meeting. I think it's a good move and doubt I'll go either. **Bad:** You're right. I'm not going either.

9. When you forward an FYI email, provide a summary rather than assuming the recipient will take the time to read it all and figure out what's going on.

When you're the recipient:

1. Be careful about making assumptions about the emotions behind a message. Email and emotions are rife with misunderstandings. Unless the sender spells out that he or she is angry with you, don't jump to that conclusion. When you receive an email that concerns you, wait an hour or so and read it again. In fact, walk away from it for as long as you're able. Check to see if there's another way to interpret the message.

2. Do not escalate a conflict by sending an emotionally charged reply.

3. Ask for details or a clarification.

4. Most email programs have excellent built-in tools to organize messages. Use them to your benefit.

5. Unless you are being paid solely to send and receive emails, you don't have to respond to every message right away. Give yourself permission to finish other activities before you respond. Some people even schedule email time and check their email at various intervals throughout the day.

5.16 Planning

The process of annual planning for most teams requires assessment of results delivered in the previous year and the team's work practices to identify areas of improvement. It requires a clear goal and common purpose for the team to achieve and the initiatives and tactics required to get there. (See OGSM information in previous chapters.)

5.17 Team time-out

A coach calls a time out when he or she feels performance is waning or when it's worth taking a step back to give players a breather—maybe it's to celebrate successes or pre-empt a lull.

During this time-out, consider this definition of insanity: doing the same thing over and over again and expecting different results.

Is your team repeating the same practices or processes and continuing to expect different results? Evaluate the situation. Pinpoint the problem. Develop a new process to improve results. Remember, left unattended, workflow morphs and spreads to people who get the work done—creating over-worked and under-worked team members. Take this time-out and step back and ensure that your team is working efficiently.

Create your own best practices.

NOTES:

> ❝**Employ thy time well, if thou meanest to gain leisure.**❞
>
> – Benjamin Franklin

Summary
Chapter 5: Efficient Practices

1. **Planning Horizons:** The team has an effective approach to planning both short and long-term.

2. **Prioritizing:** The team has a clear process to identify and manage priorities.

3. **Resource allocation:** The team is effective at resource planning and making necessary adjustments based on changing priorities.

4. **Core work processes:** The team has key work processes that are well defined, written and practiced.

5. **Meetings:** Team members consider meetings both effective *(we get stuff done)* and efficient *(we're mindful of time as a critical resource).*

6. **Problem solving:** The team is successful at defining the problem, identifying root cause, clarifying options and making decisions.

7. **Continuous improvement:** The team regularly reviews and consistently improves business practices.

8. **Communication:** The team's communication process can be defined as open, direct, timely and accurate.

9. **Conflict resolution:** The team has an effective approach to managing conflict both internally and with others outside the team.

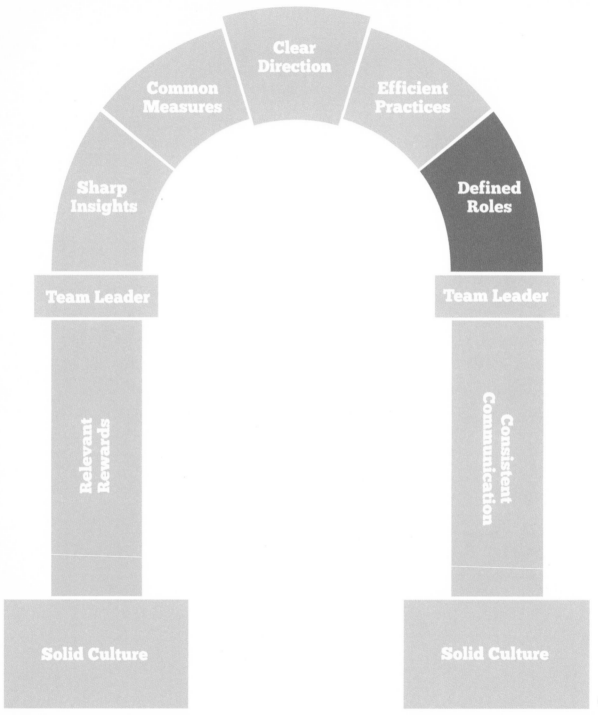

Defined Roles

When the Space Shuttle Challenger lifted off January 28, 1986, the whole world watched the result of the thousands of individual efforts coming together to create an incredible machine. Moments later, when the Challenger exploded, the world saw the high-stakes consequences of the tragic decision to launch that morning.

Crew member Christa McAuliffe, the first Space Shuttle passenger participating in the NASA Teacher in Space Program, had planned to conduct live educational broadcasts, transmitted to classrooms throughout the world during the mission. Her place on the shuttle symbolized a new era for NASA.

Pinpointing the cause of the explosion didn't take long. In fact, Roger Boisjoly, a Morton Thiokol engineer, believed he knew exactly what the problem was from the moment it occurred. For months leading up to the launch, Boisjoly repeatedly attempted to call attention to the craft's faulty O-rings.

> ## 66 Whenever you do a thing, act as if all the world were watching. 99
>
> ### – Thomas Jefferson

From the time he started working for NASA in 1980—after every launch, according to Boisjoly—he and other Morton Thiokol engineers retrieved the rocket fuel cylinders to prepare them for the next flight. When he and his team inspected the O-rings following a January 1985 launch—one year before the tragedy occurred—the engineers found that the O-rings were not functioning properly. Large amounts of fuel had escaped past the primary seal. Boisjoly recognized the problem was so severe that the January 1985 launch had probably missed ending in disaster by seconds.

After his findings, Boisjoly and other engineers found that the rings had trouble sealing at 53 degrees Fahrenheit or below. They determined that if the primary seal was destroyed, the back-up seal had a great chance of failing—"close to 100 percent chance of destruction," Boisjoly has repeatedly said in the years since.

Initially, Boisjoly's managers asked the engineering team to keep the information that the rings had trouble sealing at or below 53 degrees a secret, according to Boisjoly. However, he refused to keep quiet and at a presentation about the faultiness of the O-rings with NASA, Morton Thiokol officials decided to tell NASA what they had learned.

According to public documents analyzing the Challenger disaster, immediately after Morton Thiokol's presentation to NASA, most of the decision-makers believed Morton Thiokol engineers' concerns were valid enough to cancel the launch. However, when the real decision-making time came, only selected senior officials were allowed to be involved. None of the engineers who knew firsthand what happened at 53 degrees were consulted.

Many believe a combination of political and economic factors pressured decision-makers to continue full steam ahead.

The night before the Challenger launch, Florida experienced record low temperatures. Knowing what temperatures in the high teens and low 20s could mean for the Challenger,

Morton Thiokol engineers, including Boisjoly, formed a stop-launch group and met with their chain of command. During the meeting, according to Boisjoly, he and his colleagues were able to persuade superiors to stop the flight. But when Morton Thiokol informed NASA to stop the launch, NASA's upper management asked for an immediate meeting with Morton Thiokol in 45 minutes. Public documents show that because the Shuttle launch had already been delayed several times due to weather, many top-level NASA decision makers viewed canceling another launch as out of the question.

When NASA requested a definitive recommendation from Morton Thiokol, representatives pushed for a delayed launch until the outside air temperature reached 53 degrees. Public documents show that NASA manager Lawrence Mulloy responded to the recommendation by asking, "My God, Thiokol, when do you want me to launch, next April?"

Finally, under significant pressure from NASA, Morton Thiokol managers gave the go-ahead for launch.

At launch time, the temperature at Cape Canaveral was 29 degrees. Boisjoly has said he had a sense of relief when the shuttle didn't explode on the pad as he had predicted. Seconds later, all hopes for a successful mission were lost.

Following the Challenger disaster, both NASA and Morton Thiokol initially denied any pre-disaster knowledge of the faulty O-rings. Boisjoly, however, testified against them. In the years that followed, Boisjoly has said he paid a high price for his decision to speak out. However, he has also said that he would do it all again.

He was, after all, doing the job he was tasked to do.

6.2 Lessons learned from Challenger

The devastating story of the Challenger disaster demonstrates why deferring to competency is critical to the success of a team—and, ultimately, the organization as a whole.

The moral of the Challenger story is that if the right people are doing the right jobs on a team, the right thing to do is to listen to them. Trusting people on the team is imperative in the Team Arch®.

The team member who knows the most about a particular topic needs to be the one making the decision. It's about trust and having competent people in place. The best management always defaults to competency. Poor management overrides competency—and that decision almost always leads to poor results, and sometimes leads to disastrous and tragic results as in the Space Shuttle Challenger accident.

6.3 Push decisions down

Boisjoly was crystal clear about his defined tasks—to the point of not listening when supervisors asked him to keep quiet about the problem he had found with the O-rings. His managers also failed to listen, but somewhere along the way, someone had done a good job of giving Boisjoly defined tasks. That clear direction remained his focus.

The first step toward empowering individual team members to do their jobs and to have the follow-through required to complete the goal successfully is to be certain each team member understands his or her defined tasks.

A successful manager breaks down the work process so clearly that each team member fully understands the consequences—a crumbling process—if he or she doesn't complete his or her defined tasks. There is no magic potion for making each team member understand his or her responsibilities. A team leader is charged with divvying out the tasks based on capability, competency and capacity.

6.4 We have a problem

If a company or team isn't achieving the results it's after, change is necessary. To get different results, the work must also be changed. The team leader has to ask The Big Question: What is keeping us from achieving the results we're trying to get?

The Big Question leads to seven other critical questions:

1. **People.** Does the team have the skills to do the work required?

2. **Process.** Is the team working as efficiently as possible? Are there breakdowns in the way the team is working?

3. **Information.** Does the team have the necessary data to make quality decisions?

4. **Governance.** Are the decision criteria clear? Is the decision-maker clear? Are decisions being made at the right points along the process?

5. **Rewards.** Is the team incenting people to get the right behavior?

6. **Measures.** Is the team measuring the right things?

7. **Structure.** Does the organization design best deliver value to the market?

The team leader and team must be vigilant in accessing and re-evaluating the roles and resources available to get work done. Part of the task is about clearly defining the competencies needed on the team to deliver the work. Once a clear direction has been set and work has been defined, the team can proceed toward the goal. The interdependency of the team and its skills cannot be separated from accomplishing the overall goal.

When roles and tasks are left undefined, there is a lack of clarity in job responsibilities, accountability and decision-making—which all leads to conflict and confusion.

ROLES AND DECISION RIGHTS

A lot of successful organizations use a role description and decision matrix called RACI to help clarify roles and responsibilities. RACI is an acronym, which stands for:

 Responsible: For every decision made in the organization, someone is responsible for making it.

 Accountable: In most cases, in a hierarchical organization, someone can overrule the decision. (In some cases in some organizations, the R and the A can be the same person.)

 Consulted: People who may have critical information that could be helpful in making the decision, but it's not their decision to make.

 Informed: The team members informed of the decision.

Someone is responsible for making every decision in an organization. Unless the decision comes from the very top of the organization, in a hierarchical organization, someone can overrule every decision. A good role description will clarify job responsibilities and key decision rights. It will specify work responsibilities and include success measures.

These tools are simple and help team members understand their roles, decisions and deliverables. A successful team does not allow people to retreat into their isolated roles and responsibilities. The team, as a whole, requires everyone to work together. The integrated relationships created by a team offer a starting place for discussions of what's working and what isn't.

	VP Global BU	Global Segment Leader	Global Product Manager	Global R&D Director	Global MK Director	GM Region	Regional Segment Manager	Regional Product Manager (Portfolio)	Sales Director
Who determines the pricing process that the Division will follow?	A				R	C	C	C	I
Who executes pricing within the business rules?	I	I	I	I	I	A	C	R	C
Who decides on a price increase?	A	R	C	C	C	R	I	I	I
Who decides on end user global project planning?	A	R	C	C	C	R	I	I	I
Who decides on rebates?			I	I		A	C	C	R
Who owns product warranties?	I	I	A			C	C	R	C
Who sets the pricing business rules for segments?		A	R			I	I	I	I

RACI EXAMPLE: Decision Matrix for a global manufacturer

> **66** It's just a job. Grass grows, birds fly, waves pound the sand. I beat people up. **99**
>
> – Muhammad Ali

6.6 Understanding job responsibilities

Delineating job responsibilities for each team member is not complex, but empowering team members to take responsibility for their assigned tasks and implement them with other team members is like parenting. It takes an incredible balance of providing enough support, coupled with enough room for independence, for personal accountability to flourish.

First and clearly, each person needs to have a role on the team. The most embraced route to divvying up responsibilities is for the team leader to consider the skills and roles required for the team to accomplish its goals. Then, the team leader needs to match those roles to the known capabilities of the team members, carefully distributing the work and not overloading individual members. This pairing of team members with defined tasks forces the team leader to observe what people are best at doing. Evaluating success and results along the way is necessary and could lead to changes in roles and responsibilities.

6.7 A different approach to divvying up work responsibilities

Another effective way is to set the task in front of the team and allow them to define their own roles and responsibilities. That way, members can collectively view the challenge, offer their own skills and debate who is best suited to fill each of the core roles. This builds a sense of cohesion and a deep understanding of what each member is required to do for the team to be successful.

> ❝**Everybody has talent, it's just a matter of moving around until you've discovered what it is.**❞
>
> – George Lucas

6.8 Finding the right skills

Finding the right skills requires a team to assess its true capability and determine who is capable of best helping them win in a certain area. Once actual work begins, members' strengths will become more apparent. Watching people discover hidden talents or abilities is incredibly gratifying—and one of the many reasons why everyone should be encouraged and given the opportunity to stretch.

One factor to consider in determining which team members should help in which area is that many people do not know what they have until they are pushed into giving it all.

Sports often demonstrate this well. Whether it is basketball, football, hockey or even relay races, analyzing the other team members and playing to one's strengths is an effective approach.

6.9 Dealing with internal competition

Internal competition, however, is one of the most destructive forces on a team. It can thwart a team's ability to compete against the challenge by pitting team members against each other. Team members vie for position, as if someone will be eliminated from the team.

Team members must know that they each have a place on the team—and that place is of value to the team. Even though this understanding seems basic, some team members need more assurance than others that their place and work—in and on the team—is valued. Team members also need varying degrees of assurance that the team leader will be fair and unbiased in assessments and managing the team.

The team leader then has to be fair and unbiased. Missteps along that path will counteract months of good work done and add to any previous concerns of internal competition.

The team leader must make the performance goals, deliverables and values clear in order for the members to operate fairly and effectively. With the right team members and structure, internal and individual competition will—and must—give way to collective performance. That is what will guarantee success and the rewards that come with it.

6.10 Comfortable governance

As with so many teamwork dynamics, comfortable governance is a trust issue. Team members must be comfortable that the team leader has the vision to lead and guide a team to success.

Comfortable governance requires a certain amount of patience and time. A team leader may ask, "How do I continue to give a certain team member the opportunity to demonstrate the competency to make the decision?"

Trust is a two-way street. A team leader also has to learn to accept the way some team members work. Getting to a place of, "Just because it's not my way, doesn't mean it doesn't work," is critical to being an effective leader.

Take for example, when a team member is asked to build a presentation. Perhaps the way the presentation was developed was not exactly what the team leader would have done. But, the question is, "Does the presentation accomplish what needed to be accomplished and is it effective?"

Too many managers justify their existence by making minor changes to subordinates' work. Effective managers set direction and expectations of output and let their people deliver. Many times a growing manager will ask, "Does making that change to the subordinate's work add any value to the equation?"

Determining the sweet spot in governance is complex and multifaceted. Pushing down a decision to its lowest point in an organization contributes to that organization's overall effectiveness. But it's not an easy process. For example, how many organizations struggle with determining what size budget a mid-level manager or sales executive may approve without seeking permission from the level above? In many situations, an organization simply can't pick an arbitrary number. Every organization has to make that decision as to what level to push that decision.

> **66 All organizations are perfectly designed to get the results they are now getting. If we want different results, we must change the way we do things. 99**
>
> – Tom Northup

6.11 Clear expectations and prioritization

Nothing brings a team closer together than winning. When a team earns an early win, members get a sense of accomplishment. With wind in their sails, they continue to perform at a high level.

For teams to continue winning, team leaders must walk the tight rope. They must continually review prioritization, but they must also deliver a message consistent enough to keep team members believing in what they're doing.

They have to regularly review job performance while constantly demonstrating trust in each individual team member's performance. It's a never-ending tightrope, but the payoff is big.

At the end of the day, the best way for a manager to work is to create an even keel. Good managers know not to create massive highs and massive lows. They have to stay in a constant assessor mode and give their team reasonable milestones to celebrate. Teams, like individuals, need positive reinforcement. Successful team leaders often manage by calling attention to individual achievements.

A team leader's goal is to create positive momentum.

> **"If it's your job to eat a frog, it's best to do it first thing in the morning. And if it's your job to eat two frogs, it's best to eat the biggest one first."**
>
> **– Mark Twain**

Summary
Chapter 6: Defined Roles

1. **Defined responsibilities:** Each team member understands his or her job responsibilities.

2. **Big picture:** The team members understand how their work links with other team members and work processes.

3. **Ownership:** Each team member takes responsibility for getting the work done—or not.

4. **Competency:** The team has the right skills to accomplish our goals.

5. **Leverage:** The team fully utilizes the skills, knowledge and experience of team members.

6. **Clear expectations:** The team leader clearly sets work expectations for each team member.

7. **Decision rights:** Team members know the decisions they should make and the decisions others should make.

8. **Decision level:** Decisions are made at the appropriate level in the organization.

9. **Regulated and balanced:** Team members' roles and workload are regularly reviewed, prioritized and balanced, in accordance with team goals.

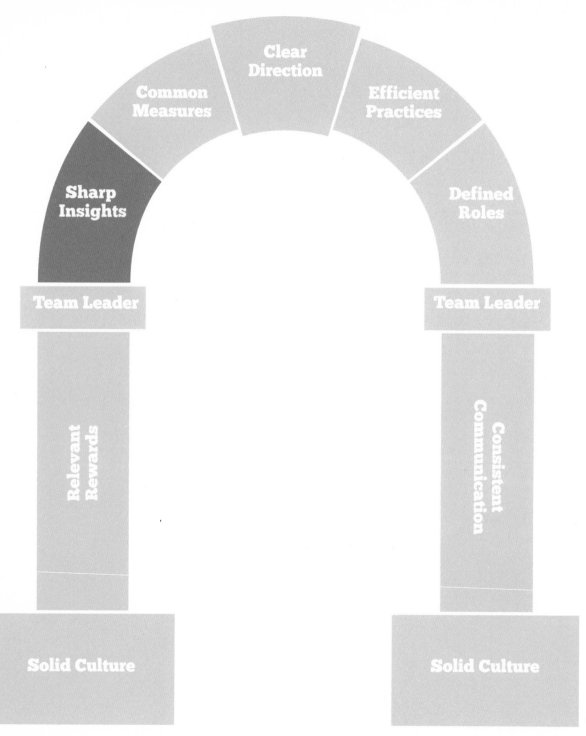

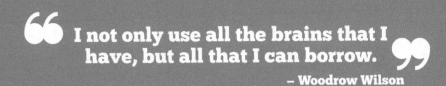

> ## 66 I not only use all the brains that I have, but all that I can borrow. 99
>
> – Woodrow Wilson

Sharp Insights

Think they've already thought of everything? Think again.

Woody Norris is a modern day Thomas Edison. What Edison did for light, Norris is doing for sound—and though his inventions have made him millions, he continues to live a relatively quiet life as a serial inventor.

His electronics training began when he was a kid in Maryland. As the son of a coal miner with a third-grade education, Norris repaired broken radios and learned everything he could about electronics. When he won the Lemelson-MIT Award in 2005, the committee described Norris as, "a classic independent inventor, Norris is self-educated, self-funded and self-motivated."

Norris always seems to be thinking and staying one step ahead of the game, but not so far ahead of the rest of us, that we can't apply his inventions to our lives.

For example, one weekend back in 1967, Norris utilized Doppler technology to create a sonar tool that isolated movements inside the human body. That weekend's work led to the sonogram.

> ❝ **Any intelligent fool can make things bigger and more complex... It takes a touch of genius—and a lot of courage to move in the opposite direction.** ❞
>
> **–Albert Einstein**

More recently, Norris has been working on his HyperSonic Sound (HSS®) invention—a completely different kind of speaker system that directs sound. At a speech for TED, the bi-annual global gathering of geniuses organized to disseminate "ideas worth spreading," Norris demonstrated using an HSS about the size of a piece of legal paper—and not a whole lot thicker. HSS focuses sound like a laser beam—and the people not in the beam of sound, even a few inches away, cannot hear it.

He's also created the AirScooter®, a single person helicopter that you can learn to fly in a half-hour. He predicts the invention could change the world.

In the 1980s, NASA asked Norris to help with a replacement for the built-in microphones in astronaut's helmets. Norris used the principle that sound travels through bones to create a hands-free ear-mounted speaker/microphone device. Chances are you didn't know about that—but have you ever seen or used a Bluetooth headset? Yep, Norris came up with that idea too.

The list keeps going and going. With more than 40 U.S. patents in hand and dozens more pending, Norris gathers data to inspire his creations—things the rest of us will be ready for in the future. His work demonstrates the extreme in gathering data, connecting the dots and producing brilliance.

What Norris and his inventions show is the necessity for a willingness to tinker. He is the epitome of intellectual curiosity in this day and age. Good insight comes from people who are curious.

7.2 Turning information into insights

There's a difference between information and insights. Accessing good data is becoming easier, but reaching insights requires a genuine curiosity—a team must be interested and willing to tinker. Insight is what moves a team to action.

A team is an open system by nature, gaining information from various directions and different inputs. The Team Arch® model helps effective teams pull out insightful nuggets from data and move on. If not, they get stuck in analysis paralysis.

If a team squeezes data hard enough, eventually the data will scream—leading to new notions, ideas and theories. For example, organizing data in meaningful chunks, using graphs or charts often helps team members draw comparisons and conclusions and identify trends.

A team's goal is to figure out why data is behaving in a certain way. Good analytics bring data to life. The data needs to be pushed and pulled by different forces. The team's job is to understand the forces pushing the data so that insights can be gleaned and plans built to improve the performance of the team.

Data has movement. It tells a story. A team has to figure out what the story is and why the story is being told.

Often teams consider data as numbers only, but there are other forms of data that are sometimes forgotten. For example, there is an inherent understanding of how things work (natural laws, principles and physics) and how they have worked in the past (models, unforeseen consequences and historic trends).

Gut instinct is rarely arbitrary. Gut instinct is built on truth, experience, history and perspective—a composite of the person. The right composite leads to insight. Even intuition is based upon understanding how things should work or taking into account more than the traditional data set.

Lots of people looked at the exact Doppler technology Norris studied, but Norris saw its use for other things.

7.3 Watch Out

Be careful not to ignore yellow caution lights. The strongest teams are mindful of insights that are counterintuitive. Sometimes literally "sleeping on" a big decision is critical.

Maarten Bos, a social psychologist and researcher at Radboud University in the Netherlands, published results in 2011 from an experiment that offered new insights on the underlying mechanisms of making complex decisions. His results show that, in fact, sleeping on a complex decision is often the best means of making the best decision. His research shows that our brains continue to process data and information when we're not consciously thinking about the situation.

When the mind is distracted on another task, especially mindless tasks, or when the mind is not consciously focused on an issue (for example during sleep), an active process in the brain accurately evaluates the pros and cons of relevant decision attributes.

In Bos' experiment, participants were presented with information about cars. "Some cars possessed many positive but irrelevant attributes, whereas others possessed fewer positive, but important attributes. Those participants who decided immediately chose the cars with many but unimportant attributes, whereas participants who were first given a task to distract them from the decision chose the quality cars. In short, sleeping on a decision allows us to differentiate between the vital and the irrelevant aspects, ultimately leading to higher quality decisions. The unconscious can process large amounts of information—as long as we give it time to do so." (Harvard Business Review Blog Network, May 16, 2011)

7.4 Insights—getting data to scream

To turn data into useful insights, a team needs a clear understanding of the situation and its moving parts, including how the data was gathered and what weaknesses the data may have. The team also needs members who have the ability to assimilate data from various sources—beyond numbers.

The fundamental dilemma is that data on its own does not tell much. Teams need to arrange data into a logical pattern to see how things are related. Interpretations require looking at the data from perspectives until it actually reveals a pattern—a series of results that can be correlated. Once organized and visually displayed, data shows how things work.

Many teams and team leaders stop there. They read the data but cannot make the data tell a story. Once a team understands the patterns data creates, they can break it into pieces—and just like an erector set—rebuild it so others can understand it.

7.5 Willingness to go deeper

The big challenge of quantitative analysis is that two people can look at the same data and come up with two different conclusions. Teams need to remember that a single data point is perspective. Multiple data points are truth.

The most insightful analytical material is created when a team is willing to go the extra mile in corroborating potential insights with different data. The worst analysis takes data, draws simple conclusions and puts those conclusions out as truth.

> **Learning to make films is very easy. Learning what to make films about is very hard.**
> —George Lucas

Again, teams must be aware that weaknesses in analysis occur when they mistakenly believe data lies 100 percent in numbers. Data comes in multiple shapes and forms. Interviewing a customer becomes data. Analyzing a sales trend is data. Customer service feedback and seemingly unrelated market observations can serve as data.

With modern technology, teams have more industry research at their fingertips than ever before. But just because more information is out there doesn't mean a team knows more. In fact, more information may mean teams know less because the bombardment of data can be overwhelming. The team's process of collecting, organizing and synthesizing information is critical.

WANTED: Different thinking styles

Every team needs a variety of different thinkers to look at problems and opportunities from different perspectives. Though there are many nuances and mechanisms of divvying up thinking styles, most generally, thinkers fall into four basic categories:

Innovators strategic, creative, visionary
Analyzers logical, quantitative, factual
Planners sequential, organized, structured
Connectors interpersonal, compassionate, empathetic

With too many of any one type in a room, the team will get off balance and miss opportunities and solutions. For example, if a team were bringing a product to market, it would need all four thinking styles to be most successful. Rich, the innovator, would automatically ask: Are we the first ones to ever do this? Where could this product take our company? What channels, customers and markets would this give us the opportunity to penetrate? How does this product support the image of our brand? Jackie, the analyzer, would automatically ask: How much money are we going to make? How many sales can we generate? How will this help us grow our market share?

Stephanie, the planner, would ask: How are we going to get this done? Who's going to do what? What are our priorities? What if this fails? Has anyone ever launched a product like this before? What were the results? What are our benchmarks? Tom, the connector, would ask: Will our customers like this product? Do our customers need this product? What would make more customers want this product?

To offer further insight into thinking styles, take the example of purchasing a new car. Perhaps all four people want the same car, but their reasons for wanting it differ greatly.

Rich, the innovative thinker, would want the new car because it's sleek. It's got state-of-the-art technology with auto-assist parking, the latest and greatest connectivity and an ahead-of-its-time transmission. Plus, it's the first electric car that goes 0 to 60 in less than eight seconds and lasts for three hours on one charge. Jackie, the analyzer, will want the same car because it costs less than $30,000, and the gas savings will cover the costs of insurance. After much thorough research, she knows this car is the best value on the road today. Stephanie, the planner, recognizes that this car comes with a seven-year limited warranty and lifetime electronics support. Plus, it was voted the best electric car by *Consumer Reports*. Tom, the connector, knows this car is the right thing to do for the environment. It sends the right message to his kids, and it's big enough to use to drive customers around town.

The bottom line:

Every team needs different styles of thinkers to work to its best—innovators, analyzers, planners and connectors. Teams that incorporate different types of thinking learn to recognize the value of other people's perspectives—which ends up making them more successful.

7.7
STEPS TO INCREASE ANALYTICAL SKILLS

A team can take a number of steps to improve and increase its base of analytical skills.

1. Taking a skills inventory can boost morale and serve as a wake-up call for those who tend to think in terms of black and white. It also happens to function as a good team exercise. In most cases, teams and team leaders are surprised by the skills their own people possess. Just remember, if a required skill is very specialized, it may be more cost-effective to outsource it.

2. Focus on the critical skills necessary to accomplish the team's destination.

3. Train the team in basic data analysis to create a baseline for the team of analytical skills.

4. Assign the work to a team member with the skills and apply them to the tasks that need to be done.

5. Collectively brainstorm the data with the team for observations and insights.

6. If necessary, augment the team with people who have the skills the team needs to succeed.

7. If the team still needs help to accomplish its goal, develop, hire or outsource the needed skills.

8. Twice a year, a team should look at the work of the preceding six months and discuss the skills inventory, compare the work to the skills and make adjustments.

9. As new members join the team, update and revise your skills inventory.

7.8 Skills inventory

People have hidden and not-so-hidden talents—and they generally love being recognized for talents that may be under-utilized or unknown in a work environment. Using a team member to his or her fullest potential is a win-win for everyone. However, too often managers and team members tend to box people into set roles.

Giving team members the opportunity to use and be recognized for skills they may not have been hired to do creates affirming growth within a team. Use a skills inventory, such as the one included here, to pinpoint skill sets team members may have. This skills inventory includes a variety of skills that cover a wide range. Ask team members to review and mark the list of varied skills. When reviewing the inventory, note clusters of skills. For the most honest and accurate feedback, ask team members to be prepared to provide a real example of how they used a noted skill successfully. Once team members have completed the inventory, ask them to review it a final time to identify and highlight the skills they like to use.

Group A				
Public speaking	Not a skill	Basic	Intermediate	Master
Business writing	Not a skill	Basic	Intermediate	Master
Creative writing	Not a skill	Basic	Intermediate	Master
Persuading	Not a skill	Basic	Intermediate	Master
Editing	Not a skill	Basic	Intermediate	Master
Interviewing	Not a skill	Basic	Intermediate	Master
Summarizing/influencing	Not a skill	Basic	Intermediate	Master

Group B				
Relating well to others	Not a skil	Basic	Intermediate	Master
Building teams and alliances	Not a skill	Basic	Intermediate	Master
Negotiating agreements	Not a skill	Basic	Intermediate	Master
Settling disagreements	Not a skill	Basic	Intermediate	Master
Persuading and guiding	Not a skill	Basic	Intermediate	Master
Selling ideas/promoting	Not a skill	Basic	Intermediate	Master

Observing	Not a skill	Basic	Intermediate	Master
Identifying trends	Not a skill	Basic	Intermediate	Master
Synthesizing	Not a skill	Basic	Intermediate	Master
Analyzing/assessing	Not a skill	Basic	Intermediate	Master
Retaining facts & details	Not a skill	Basic	Intermediate	Master
Learns by doing	Not a skill	Basic	Intermediate	Master
Learns by reading	Not a skill	Basic	Intermediate	Master
Learns by watching	Not a skill	Basic	Intermediate	Master
Learns by listening	Not a skill	Basic	Intermediate	Master
Extrapolating to other situations	Not a skill	Basic	Intermediate	Master

Managing self	Not a skill	Basic	Intermediate	Master
Setting priorities	Not a skill	Basic	Intermediate	Master
Identifying direction	Not a skill	Basic	Intermediate	Master
Working without supervision	Not a skill	Basic	Intermediate	Master
Accepting responsibility	Not a skill	Basic	Intermediate	Master
Delegating	Not a skill	Basic	Intermediate	Master
Monitoring progress	Not a skill	Basic	Intermediate	Master
Managing meetings/conferences	Not a skill	Basic	Intermediate	Master
Identifying problems and solutions	Not a skill	Basic	Intermediate	Master
Managing up and down the organization	Not a skill	Basic	Intermediate	Master
Adapting to new situations	Not a skill	Basic	Intermediate	Master
Building teams	Not a skill	Basic	Intermediate	Master
Working well independently	Not a skill	Basic	Intermediate	Master
Motivating others	Not a skill	Basic	Intermediate	Master
Guiding and coaching	Not a skill	Basic	Intermediate	Master
Demonstrating integrity and values	Not a skill	Basic	Intermediate	Master
Working Hard	Not a skill	Basic	Intermediate	Master

Group D Continued				
Detail-oriented	Not a skill	Basic	Intermediate	Master
Delivering results	Not a skill	Basic	Intermediate	Master
Managing conflict	Not a skill	Basic	Intermediate	Master
Storytelling	Not a skill	Basic	Intermediate	Master
Curiousity	Not a skill	Basic	Intermediate	Master

Group E				
Listening	Not a skill	Basic	Intermediate	Master
Identifying personal growth areas	Not a skill	Basic	Intermediate	Master
Providing instruction/input	Not a skill	Basic	Intermediate	Master
Creating learning opportunities	Not a skill	Basic	Intermediate	Master
Facilitating group process	Not a skill	Basic	Intermediate	Master
Encouraging/guiding	Not a skill	Basic	Intermediate	Master
Designing curriculum	Not a skill	Basic	Intermediate	Master
Facilitating	Not a skill	Basic	Intermediate	Master
Advising/coaching one on one	Not a skill	Basic	Intermediate	Master

Group F				
Constructing	Not a skill	Basic	Intermediate	Master
Handling	Not a skill	Basic	Intermediate	Master
Installing	Not a skill	Basic	Intermediate	Master
Cooking	Not a skill	Basic	Intermediate	Master
Operating tools/machines	Not a skill	Basic	Intermediate	Master
Producing	Not a skill	Basic	Intermediate	Master
Repairing/restoring	Not a skill	Basic	Intermediate	Master
Gardening	Not a skill	Basic	Intermediate	Master
Designing	Not a skill	Basic	Intermediate	Master

Setting goals/priorities	Not a skill	Basic	Intermediate	Master
Executing projects	Not a skill	Basic	Intermediate	Master
Delegating	Not a skill	Basic	Intermediate	Master
Following through	Not a skill	Basic	Intermediate	Master
Building alliances/teams	Not a skill	Basic	Intermediate	Master
Anticipating problems	Not a skill	Basic	Intermediate	Master
Scheduling	Not a skill	Basic	Intermediate	Master
Responding	Not a skill	Basic	Intermediate	Master
Evaluating	Not a skill	Basic	Intermediate	Master
Operating under stress	Not a skill	Basic	Intermediate	Master
Assuring quality	Not a skill	Basic	Intermediate	Master
Recommending	Not a skill	Basic	Intermediate	Master
Forecasting	Not a skill	Basic	Intermediate	Master
Computer literate	Not a skill	Basic	Intermediate	Master
Coordinating	Not a skill	Basic	Intermediate	Master
Organizing	Not a skill	Basic	Intermediate	Master
Planning	Not a skill	Basic	Intermediate	Master
Filing	Not a skill	Basic	Intermediate	Master
Stamina/endurance	Not a skill	Basic	Intermediate	Master

Noticing beauty/aesthetics	Not a skill	Basic	Intermediate	Master
Designing visually	Not a skill	Basic	Intermediate	Master
Designing materials	Not a skill	Basic	Intermediate	Master
Symbolic thinking	Not a skill	Basic	Intermediate	Master
Creating/shaping things	Not a skill	Basic	Intermediate	Master
Performing	Not a skill	Basic	Intermediate	Master
Interrelating materials/themes	Not a skill	Basic	Intermediate	Master
Improvising	Not a skill	Basic	Intermediate	Master
Listening	Not a skill	Basic	Intermediate	Master

Problem solving	Not a skill	Basic	Intermediate	Master
Sympathetic	Not a skill	Basic	Intermediate	Master
Helping	Not a skill	Basic	Intermediate	Master
Accepting	Not a skill	Basic	Intermediate	Master
Forming good rapport	Not a skill	Basic	Intermediate	Master
Mediating	Not a skill	Basic	Intermediate	Master
Handling problems/complaints	Not a skill	Basic	Intermediate	Master
Providing service	Not a skill	Basic	Intermediate	Master

Noticing trends	Not a skill	Basic	Intermediate	Master
Developing new approaches	Not a skill	Basic	Intermediate	Master
Demonstrating foresight	Not a skill	Basic	Intermediate	Master
Experimenting	Not a skill	Basic	Intermediate	Master
Adapting ideas	Not a skill	Basic	Intermediate	Master
Tolerating lack of structure	Not a skill	Basic	Intermediate	Master
Creating	Not a skill	Basic	Intermediate	Master
Imagining	Not a skill	Basic	Intermediate	Master

Math computation	Not a skill	Basic	Intermediate	Master
Using statistics	Not a skill	Basic	Intermediate	Master
Identifying trends	Not a skill	Basic	Intermediate	Master
Problem solving	Not a skill	Basic	Intermediate	Master
Accounting	Not a skill	Basic	Intermediate	Master
Estimating	Not a skill	Basic	Intermediate	Master
Financial planning	Not a skill	Basic	Intermediate	Master
Budgeting	Not a skill	Basic	Intermediate	Master

Skills Inventory Recap

Top five personal strengths:

_____

_____

_____

_____

_____

Top five skills that evoke the most joy:

_____

_____

_____

_____

_____

Top five surprise skills for each team member:

_____

_____

_____

_____

_____

_____

_____

_____

_____

_____

There is no secret code to evaluating a skills accessory. Once team members complete the survey, a team may choose to spend time as a group reviewing team members' responses—looking for surprises and possibilities of filling skills gaps. If a team takes the time to complete a skills assessment, acknowledgement in some form or fashion of the newfound skills or insights are a must—whether the skills are immediately put to use or not. Otherwise, team members are sometimes left feeling under-utilized once again.

For an element of fun, a team may even choose, in a non-work environment to host a Skills Assessment Surprise Expo, revealing the extent of their hidden talents (cooking, performing, storytelling, gardening, designing, constructing, improvising, problem solving). Activities that level the playing field create bonds that are critical to the success of a team.

7.9 Watch Out!

A word of caution to leaders: Always be careful because while data appears objective, insights gathered are subjective. Some people can make any set of data tell any story they want it to tell.

Finding the right team members with the experience and ability to integrate history, observations and the math is essential.

There's no greater predictor of the future than history. From a planning perspective, a team has to know that history is going to repeat itself unless the team does something fundamentally different. That's why finding insights is so important.

7.10
MIND THE INFORMATION GAP

1. Determine data requirements to build a complete picture early and plan internal and external data gathering as a core part of planning.

2. Be careful to allow sufficient time to gather accurate information.

3. Put funding in place to gather the right data whether from internal or external sources.

4. Familiarize yourself with what's important to key stakeholders.

5. Connect data and information to critical decision points.

7.11 Insight versus instinct

There are people who get into the executive level desks who instinctually make the best choices. Being successful as a CEO is part art, part science. Generally speaking, CEOs who fail are 100 percent art or 100 percent science.

This kind of intuition usually comes from the extrapolation of anticipated results based on models and principles that work. Intuitive leaders can be incredible at assimilating information while they anticipate and extrapolate. Like playing chess, each move is calculated based upon the potential future moves of both an organization and its competition.

7.12 A chosen path

Sometimes leaders ask teams to get data to support a specific decision. In other words, the path is chosen before the information is gathered.

Interestingly enough, the higher up in leadership, the less important data becomes. There are leaders who say, "We're going to do this because I know this is the right thing to do."

In fact, 56 percent of more than 2,000 entrepreneurs surveyed in 2011 said they relied on gut instinct when making critical decisions about a company's future, according to research by T-Mobile. Navigating the waters between cold-hard objectivity and basic instinct is often what determines success.

7.13 Analysis paralysis

To combine planning and information is vital, but teams and their leaders have to be careful not to get bogged down analyzing too much information and doing too little planning. Analysis paralysis has halted many a planning process. Balancing internal information with external information about performance is vital to good planning.

7.14 Biggest obstacle to gaining insights?

Simply put, the biggest challenge most teams have in forming sharp insights is that they become complacent and stop looking beyond their own four walls. In essence, they lose perspective because they hear opinions from the outside less and less and are told what they want to hear more and more.

NOTES:

> ## " **Genius without education is like silver in the mine.** "
>
> – Benjamin Franklin

Summary
Chapter 7: Sharp Insights

1. **Analytical skills:** The team has the analytical skills to turn data into useful insights.

2. **Productivity:** A team is able to analyze information quickly and efficiently.

3. **Increased clarity:** The team's planning process is enhanced by the effective use of information.

4. **Mining the data:** The team is capable of gathering and interpreting data.

5. **Joyful capabilities:** The team is designed with a blend of analytical skills and contentment with the work.

6. **Quality decisions:** A team's decision-making is rooted in sufficient data and insights.

7. **Moving forward:** A team avoids analysis paralysis and pushes forward through inevitable information gaps.

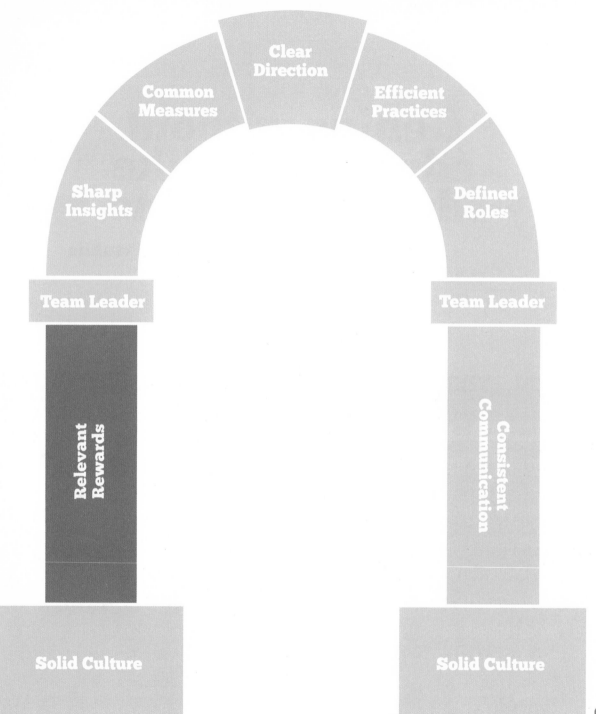

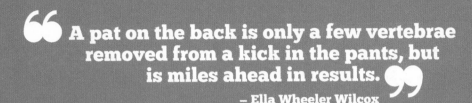
> **A pat on the back is only a few vertebrae removed from a kick in the pants, but is miles ahead in results.**
> – Ella Wheeler Wilcox

Relevant Rewards

Thoughtful parents realize that consistently rewarding one child at the expense of others does not motivate the rest to be better. Relying on individual rewards alone tends to instill a nit-picky, backbiting behavior between children.

The same is true at the corporate level.

Bob Nardelli's uninspired tenure at Home Depot is a great example of what happens when a leader over-emphasizes individual and store performance. Just like in a family with parents who consistently offer chocolate and extra allowance to the child whose chore chart has the most stars, Home Depot employees lost their team spirit and their working environment became increasingly hostile.

When Nardelli eliminated many full-time employees, masters of their fields, and replaced them with part-time employees who lacked the skills of the employees they replaced, employee morale and overall performance took another hit.

Though his decisions made fiscal sense, the end result was that Home Depot as a whole began to falter.

"A soldier will fight long and hard for a bit of colored ribbon."

–Napoleon Bonaparte

Nardelli thought people went to Home Depot simply to buy a product. In reality, they went to find a solution. The goal of the Home Depot team prior to the changes Nardelli made was to ensure a great customer experience.

Nardelli's performance at Home Depot is an example of what happens when an organization gets things wrong—specifically rewards and recognition. According to numerous reports, Nardelli's hard-driving focus on individual and store performance squashed what had previously worked well at Home Depot—a spirit of camaraderie. Employees who took pride in their work and became "experts" in specialties. More and more employees became disillusioned with each other and their work. It didn't take long for an aggressive and hostile environment to emerge. Employees, en masse, began to feel like they weren't being treated fairly.

The scenario led to Nardelli being featured on multiple lists as "the worst CEO"—a list no one wants to make.

Meanwhile, across town, around the corner or across the street, Home Depot's direct competitor, Lowe's, had a more balanced corporate culture and rewards system. On every single Lowe's receipt is a customer service survey. Lowe's has kept the emphasis on customer service. During Nardelli's tenure, Home Depot's stock price stayed stagnant, while Lowe's gained ground in the marketplace.

Nardelli missed the connection between the value of the Home Depot team's knowledge and the customer experience.

8.2
TAKE THE REWARD AND RECOGNITION CHALLENGE

So often, even the most generous team leaders can make ill-advised rewards and recognition decisions for some of their team members. For your own information and for a good reality check, take the following quiz. Then, have your team anonymously take the quiz. Compare the results. Look for the biggest gaps and lowest scores. Finally, engage the team in a conversation in what changes should be made to improve reward and recognition. Score your team on a scale from 1 ("This is not working at all on our team.") to 5 ("This is working well on our team.")

1 2 3 4 5   Our team leader doles out sincere praise when merited.

1 2 3 4 5   Our team leader recognizes team members fairly, making a point to give credit where credit is due.

1 2 3 4 5   Our team has an effective approach to resource allocation.

1 2 3 4 5   Our team members acknowledge other team members on jobs well done.

1 2 3 4 5   Our team has a formal rewards program that is transparent and consistent.

1 2 3 4 5   Our team leader understands what motivates individual team members and takes the initiative to do so.

1 2 3 4 5   Our team members understand what motivates other team members and work to create motivation for each other.

1 2 3 4 5   I feel appreciated by my team.

1 2 3 4 5   I feel fairly compensated for my work—and offered incentive to do the right thing.

1 2 3 4 5   The rewards program gives me incentive to behave in a way that is good for the company.

8.3 Driving behaviors

Organizations reward the behavior they want repeated. Rewards come three primary ways: recognition, responsibility and compensation—and those may be divided into further categories.

Company-wide reward and recognition programs have their place. So do old-fashioned and well-placed "atta-boys." Both formal and informal efforts are needed to motivate individual team members. Equally important for team leaders is the balance of individual and team recognition and rewards.

Finding the right balance of those three variables is the Holy Grail of motivation.

Like parenting, getting that equation right is complicated. It does not have a one-size fits-all solution. Even though most of us are aware of the DOs and DON'Ts of praise and recognition, a variety of factors interfere with success: Mars versus Venus? Baby Boomers versus Generation X? Management versus Frontline?

Team members approach rewards and recognition from different places. Keeping that perspective in mind is a challenge even for the most seasoned team leader. As Nardelli's tale of woe at Home Depot points out, too much focus on individual achievement creates an unhealthy environment. On the other hand, too much emphasis on team rewards creates a culture that doesn't provide incentives for most individuals to push themselves to achieve great things.

Difficult though it may be, the process of rewards and recognition establishes the culture of a team. If team leaders consistently call out individual performance, then team members will consistently strive for individual performance, sometimes at the expense of the team goal. If team leaders consistently recognize team achievement, most individuals have a tendency to stop trying to achieve great things on their own.

8.4 Rewards impact team performance

You get what you measure. Once a leader builds a business plan (OGSM), he or she sets the performance measures and then holds people accountable—and rewards them when they meet the mark. It's all transparent. Of course, there are different ways to reward, but the key is that the

> ## People repeat behavior that leads to flooding their brains with pleasurable chemicals.
> –Keith Henson

8.5 Watch Out

While the competitive nature of reward is important, being careful not to overly recognize a single individual's performance is critical. The issue with overly recognizing a single individual's performance is mostly the case of credit—a leader must be careful to give credit to all those responsible for a job well done.

Team members crave support from team leaders and involvement in decisions that guide the team. When a team leader asks team members for their perspectives and ideas, engages them in the decision-making process, provides them authority to accomplish their roles and responsibilities, backs them up when they make a mistake—the team leader earns loyalty and support no title will ever confer.

But the single thing most team members are looking for that doesn't cost team leaders a penny is plain and simple: Praise. Sincere praise—whether verbal, written, public or private—goes a long, long way. Time and again, research shows that the single biggest reason people feel good or bad about a job is their direct manager.

An employee isn't happy if one of the following isn't in place: He doesn't feel like his voice is heard. She doesn't believe there is a direct manager or other close co-worker who seems to care about her as a person and recognizes her for a job well done.

leader and the team members understand what good performance looks like. Strong teams set the measures, track progress, communicate often and reward performance.

Research shows that group-based incentive pay on its own raises line productivity. Working in a team system, in addition to using group incentives leads to a further productivity increase.

8.6 From the employer's perspective

A company can make the most calculated and strategic rewards choices by untangling employee objectives that are sometimes layered and conflicting. Beyond the effect an organization's rewards program has from the employee perspective, rewards can also have a positive impact on the employer. Results from effective rewards programs can be measureable and real across the board in employee engagement, health, productivity, retention and even from a public relations standpoint. From an employer perspective, a rewards program's payoff to an organization should be worth its effort when evaluated on the following criteria:

- Cost: The rewards system should benefit the employer and be worth the money or effort.

- Results: The rewards system should give incentives for employees to work and behave in a way that puts the company in a better position.

- Employee health: The rewards system should improve employee health and well-being, which in turn increases productivity and reduces sick leave.

- Retention: The rewards system should increase employee loyalty.

- Attraction: The rewards system should help recruit talented candidates.

- Implementation: The rewards system should be uncomplicated to put into place.

- Public relations: The rewards system should positively influence the organization's public image.

- Market competitiveness: The rewards system should reinforce an organization's position relative to competitors.

"An ounce of performance is worth pounds of promises."
–Mae West

8.7 Reward categories and possibilities:

Personal	Health	Professional	Money
Time off	Gym membership	Career visibility	Savings plans
Gift cards	Wellness program	Learning opportunities	Financial planning
Flexible work	Health check-ups	Professional memberships	Cash incentives
Concierge service	Disability insurance	Coaching or mentoring	Retirement contributions
Workspace	Health care options	Engaging culture	Tax prep discounts
Vacations	Healthy snacks	Responsibility	Performance bonus
Club memberships		Formal awards	Stock options
Facilitated volunteerism			
Note of thanks			

*Note: Certain kinds of rewards may incur an additional tax obligation for employees.

8.8 Making formal reward structures work

Some awards programs breed all the wrong behaviors—backbiting, tearing down, infighting and low employee morale. Formal awards programs that are too subjective don't work. Getting formal reward structures right requires transparency and consistency.

However, the programs have to be as objective and measurement-based as possible. If the final call requires a level of objectivity and fresh perspective that can't be found in the immediate working environment, bring in a panel of outside judges to make the decision. Be transparent as to who the judges are and the criteria of their decision. A simple award and

> ## "If I can't get the girl, at least give me more money."
> **–Alan Alda**

company-wide recognition goes a long way. An award coupled with a cash prize goes even further, but getting it wrong does more damage than good.

For example, a few years ago, at a Fortune 500 company, top sales performers earned high-dollar bonuses. That year the supply chain and finance departments changed the way they conducted business and massively improved the company's performance. The end result was that sales increased by 20 percent.

Who got the reward for the increase? The sales team.

The result? Major internal morale problems that led to destructive behaviors, unhappy employees and the loss of team members who had made a positive difference.

Clearly, the difference in sales performance was due to the supply chain and finance department's hard work. Yet they didn't receive proper credit or reward. Historically, sales people have been directly linked to top-line sales. Their positions require them to take an external role for the company. So they're compensated based on the marketplace. The challenge is that when all team members contribute to the success, then the reward should reflect so.

8.9 Parceling out informal praise…how?

Some managers and team leaders are blessed with the gift of perfect timing. The rest of us have to do some planning. Deciding when, where and how to offer some team members praise—even impromptu praise—may require some advance thought.

First and foremost, team leaders should know how a team member prefers to be praised. Shy folks may prefer an email as opposed to standing in front of a crowd and blushing. On the other hand, the most shy team member may be longing for his or her moment in the sun. Figuring out what works best and produces the most results requires trial and error and sometimes even a discussion with individual team members. Offering individual praise is not a one-size-fits-all proposition.

Another oft-forgotten effective form of recognition is organic peer recognition, when team members recognize other team members and let leaders know of fellow team members' accomplishments. Organic peer recognition is tricky to foster, but it's sometimes the most powerful and effective form of recognition around. Fostering a culture of peer recognition increases productivity and harmony. Some companies create reward systems that provide team leaders and team members tokens to be given to fellow employees as informal recognition and appreciation. If promoted and managed properly, these programs can be effective.

8.10 Recognition from the team leader

While corporate-wide reward and recognition programs are important, team members also need to be recognized by their team leaders and fellow team members. The timing of recognizing a team member is also important. Shamu receives a bucket full of fish immediately following a spectacular jump. The sooner a team leader acknowledges a desired performance, the stronger the message is received by the team member—and the more likely he or she is to repeat the desired performance.

Recognition is most powerful when there's a direct link to something that's being reinforced. Rolling a popcorn machine through the cubicles every Friday tends to make employees believe that, "It's Friday. I deserve popcorn." Linking the treat to something that went particularly well won't create a culture of entitlement.

Team leaders must keep such recognitions and rewards fresh and relevant. Traipsing out the popcorn machine every time there's a win won't go very far to earn the hearts and minds of team members. However, well-timed levity can go a long way in maintaining or even restoring waning productivity and/or morale.

Small tokens, like unexpected sno-cones on a summer afternoon, go a long way for certain teams. Team leaders gain more mileage with items of whimsy if they balance them with sincere shout-outs and more significant items of appreciation. When it comes to informal recognition and rewards, team leaders who take the time to get to know their teams figure out what motivates them. Then, they can get the most bang for their buck.

For a team that thrives on friendly competition, something like a go-cart race feeds competitive juices and fosters community. Recognizing that a go-cart race would work for a team requires a leader who pays attention. When it comes to effective rewards and recognition, team leaders need to strive to recognize the special skills and talents of team members and how specific team members contribute to the overall success of the team. The best team leaders know the skills of individual team members because they have first-hand knowledge of how that person works and what motivates that person to do better.

A team leader is like a coach. He or she must be close enough not only to know how a team member is performing but also to be able to give guidance on improving performance. Regular feedback is more useful than a one-shot big incentive disconnected from the daily realities. Working directly with the team offers team leaders the chance to observe how each team member affects the morale and the performance of the team, and that can be an essential thing. A team leader needs members who can work together, and when they do, they need to be recognized as contributing to the overall success.

8.11 The flip side

If a team is going to work effectively, holding team members and team leaders accountable is imperative. Everyone on the team has a responsibility to call out bad behavior—with, of course, great tact so as not to destroy the trust inside a team.

Influencing people happens in two ways: honey or vinegar. Good teams use a predominance of honey—positive incentives and productive influence rather than punitive damages. Team leaders and team members often have a default assumption regarding how people respond to one or the other. Some respond well to vinegar, but most do not. It is important to be able to exert positive influence on people, and that takes time and practice.

One side effect of not having or taking the time to do a job right is micromanaging—a control mechanism. Micromanagement has no place in the realm of most professionals—unless someone is in place who shouldn't be there. If the people on the team are talented and properly selected, then influence and honesty are all that is required to motivate them.

However, sometimes team leaders inherit less capable team members who are legacies

from days gone past. Micromanaging these team members won't solve the problem. Finding a better fit within the organization, retraining them or, if there's no better solution, firing them, is sometimes the only way out.

8.12 Can team members hold team leaders accountable?

At some level, teams have to hold their leaders accountable—which, of course, is easier said than done. Team leaders have a responsibility for setting direction and helping the team move in that direction. If they're not performing those responsibilities effectively, team dynamics begin to break down. Before the team becomes dysfunctional, teams have to rally around and say, "We need to do this differently." Team leaders have to be willing to listen to their team. Sometimes the team is wrong. Its perspective is incorrect. Often because team members don't have the whole story.

Accountability comes in calling out behavior. For example, at a team meeting, team members might say, "Our planning process is a mess. We have to clean it up." A team needs to be unified to bring an issue to the table.

Then, with the support of the team leader, the team takes action to correct the issue.

Accountability is about team leaders and team members holding each other to their agreed-upon performance measures, not about personal style. If a team creates a strong scorecard, everything is well-defined. For example, if weekly meeting attendance or tardiness is an issue, a team creates a scorecard for on-time meeting performance and publishes the weekly results. Well-managed, consistent metrics drive accountability. Conversely, poorly managed, inconsistent metrics contribute to a lack of productivity and negatively impact team morale and culture.

Most team leaders try to do the right thing, and many times team members don't have the full grasp of the scope of what a leader is trying to accomplish. Supporting leaders open the door to having others influence them. That influence can and does change the direction of their leadership.

In order to have influence on the direction of leadership, the team must:

- Listen carefully
- Gather the facts
- Develop acceptable solutions with options
- Address issues collectively

Most people look for leadership in the people around them. When they do not find it where it's supposed to be, they make it up themselves. Then, teams splinter and fracture and devolve into "sub-teams" in the midst of the team.

Most people do not have the influence or patience to "manage up" because they do not have the time to wait for change. Patient and loyal team members eventually get access to the heart of the leader and become trusted supporters/advisors.

8.13 Values in the workplace

Most people work for more than money. They get a sense of identity and accomplishment from their work. To get the most out of a team, team and organizational leaders have to put some things in place including:

- Company values and a culture that encourages team behavior
- A leadership culture that engenders volunteerism and employee engagement
- A hiring system that screens people very carefully to match corporate values
- A performance management system that coaches and promotes based on performance and values
- A reward system that makes the proper behaviors both measureable and validated
- A forum for communication and recognition of successes and the people that deliver them

8.14 Handling poor performance

Teams rely on each other. Team members expect each other to deliver on commitments made and do the work required and expected of them. All cylinders need to be performing at a high level for the objective to be achieved.

The challenge with performance management is understanding who can be developed and who can't be. Team leaders must work with the team to keep each team member abreast of where he or she stands based on performance objectives.

A team is a system. Poor performance in one area doesn't necessarily mean the problem lies with a single individual's mistake or shortcomings. Poor performance may be linked to the team's system, process or structure. Perhaps the team's system isn't supporting a specific team member's functional area. A good rule of thumb is to blame the system—not the person—until the opposite can be validated. However, when required, corrective action should be taken to address performance issues with individual team members.

8.15 The human connection

Even in their lives at work, people seek, crave and appreciate the opportunity to make a meaningful connection with another human being—whether that person is a fellow teammate, manager, subordinate, client or someone unrelated to their team. The chance to make a positive difference in someone's life doesn't come along very often. When that opportunity happens at work, it increases employee engagement and creates a positive momentum in the workforce.

Earning and offering rewards is an opportunity for team leaders, team members and organizations at large to give employees the chance to realize a meaningful connection with another person. Those connections tend to be the most memorable rewards team members earn at work.

That theory was validated in an informal survey of professionals. We asked, "What's the most relevant reward you've ever earned for a job well done at work? When was a time when you knew you were appreciated and valued for the work you do?" What follows on the next page is a smattering of real life replies.

8.16 What's the most relevant reward you've ever earned for a job well done at work?

"When I worked in human resources for a bi-national company along the border, I instituted an educational program in Mexico, teaching reading and writing to adult workers—and moving up through to grammar, middle and high school subject matter. The worker-students did the learning on their own time. The company provided tutors, books and supplies. Every year, we hosted a graduation ceremony and celebration. Two different instances come to mind as being very relevant and rewarding to me.

The first was a gentleman in his mid-sixties. During one celebratory luncheon, he approached me and thanked me for providing him the resources to learn to write. He said to me, 'This is the first time in my life that I am able to write my own name.'"

"The other was a young man who pulled me aside during another yearly graduation. He had completed his high school equivalency. We held a luncheon that year at the Florida Restaurant, which was at the time one of the nicest restaurants in Ciudad Juarez. This young man said to me, 'As a kid I used to walk by this restaurant and think one day I am going to come and eat here, and now look at me—here I am! Thank you for recognizing our achievement.' I was genuinely touched and realized that what is easy for many of us is something that others never have the opportunity to do. I have never forgotten how happy that young man was." **—Doug**

"When one of my former students contacted me recently to tell me she had written a children's book and had included me in the ones to whom she has dedicated the book!" **—Lynn**

"I used to work with a doctor in surgery who could be very difficult. He was the kind people would tiptoe around. Don't get me wrong, he's a great doctor, but he wasn't afraid to speak his mind and tell people how to get a job done right. On one very difficult case we were doing, he told me thank you and that mine was the kind of job performance he was looking for. It was nice to be thanked by someone for all the stress and work that was put into that case."
–Christy

"While working in Neonatal ICU, I took care of a baby boy who was born extremely premature. There were several times we thought we would lose him. His parents still send me Christmas cards and photos of him. That was over 20 years ago!" **–Gail**

What was your most relevant reward?

_____

_____

_____

_____

_____

_____

_____

_____

> **❝The highest reward that God gives us for good work is the ability to do better work.❞**
>
> **– Elbert Hubbard**

Summary
Chapter 8: Relevant Rewards

1. **Recognition:** Team members value and regularly recognize both individual and team performance.

2. **Accountability:** Team members hold each other accountable for delivering results.

3. **Framework:** The team has a formal rewards program that is transparent and consistent.

4. **Impact:** Rewards directly impact team performance.

5. **Compensation:** Team members believe they receive a fair balance of compensation, benefits, incentives and rewards for their work.

6. **Living values:** The team leader recognizes and rewards examples of team members who live the team's stated values.

7. **Appreciation:** Team members feel valued for their contributions.

8. **Consequences:** Poor performance earns fair and deliberate consequences.

9. **Human connections:** The team is rewarded with and takes the time to make real human connections.

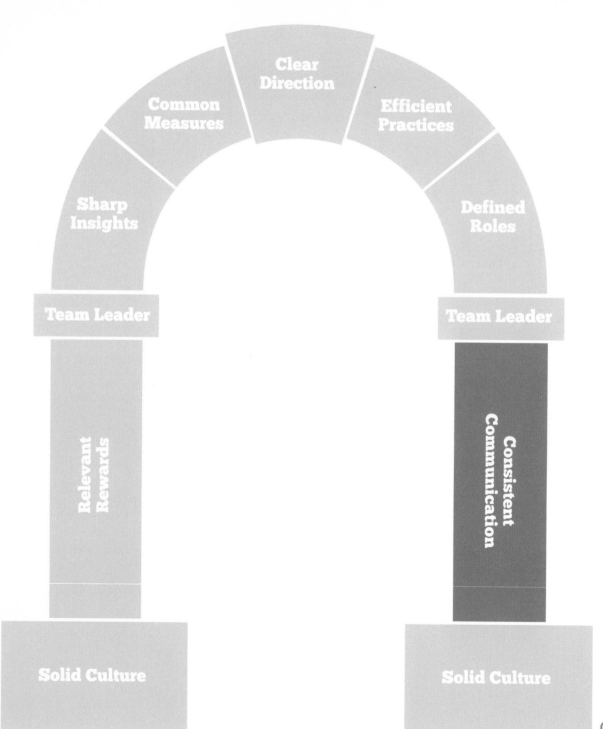

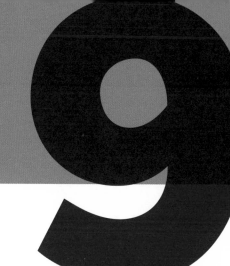

> **In the long history of humankind (and animal kind, too) those who learned to collaborate and improvise most effectively have prevailed.**
> — Charles Darwin

Consistent Communication

John Lennon and Paul McCartney collaborated for 13 years to create some of the finest and most generation-defining music of the 20th century. Their shared Liverpudlian background, combined with the early deaths of their mothers, gave them shared experiences that served as the underpinnings of the relationship they built.

McCartney was 15 when he first met Lennon, then 16, at St. Peter's Church Hall summer fete. Ivan Vaughan, a mutual friend, introduced McCartney to Lennon after The Quarrymen, Lennon's skiffle band, played for the Saturday afternoon festival in July 1957. Two weeks later, Lennon's group invited McCartney to join them—and the greatest songwriting union in the history of rock music began. George Harrison and Paul McCartney rode the same bus to school. They were friends because of a mutual interest in guitars and music. Harrison was a year younger and is said to have idolized Lennon. A year after Lennon and McCartney joined forces, they invited Harrison to join the group. Ringo joined a few years later.

"Politeness is the poison of collaboration."

– Edwin Land

They began working with Brian Epstein, a college dropout whose family owned a music store in Liverpool. Epstein handled the details and suggested group members trade their jeans for suits and ties. He helped to formalize their song line-ups during shows. All in all, he got them organized and handled the money details.

Epstein died of a drug overdose in August 1967. In John Lennon's 1970 interview with Rolling Stone magazine, he said he believed Epstein's death was the beginning of the end for the group. "I knew we were in trouble then," Lennon is quoted in the magazine.

Epstein's death left an organizational void and gave the group members the perfect opportunity to squabble.

The Beatles' growing success set the stage for individual members of the group to work toward different directions. Lennon was becoming a political superstar. Many believe that, at some level, McCartney lost trust for Lennon's intent for the band. Epstein's death created additional administrative and financial tension. Harrison didn't feel like he was getting a fair shake at songwriting. And Ringo was, well, still Ringo—the only one who ended up maintaining a good relationship with the other band members as and after the band disintegrated.

In the last years that The Beatles were technically together, in reality, they spent little time with each other. The legend goes that in late 1967, McCartney could see the writing on the walls and attempted to bring the group together by rallying the troops to get back to their roots and work together to record Let it Be, their last released album, but their second-to-last recorded album. While the music has stood the test of time, nearly three years passed between the tumultuous recording session and its release in May 1970. By comparison, less than three months passed between the recording and release of A Hard Day's Night back in 1964 when the group was more in sync.

When the Beatles broke up and each individual went off to achieve his own version of success, it was the collaboration of the group that set up the foundation of their success.

9.2 A study in trust—or the lack thereof

The Beatles began to disintegrate when they stopped communicating. For team collaboration to happen, open communication is essential. A lack of open communication creates an environment rife with the risk of conflicting agendas—and conflicting agendas destroy focus and team productivity.

Great risks to the culture of the organization occur if side conversations, hidden agendas or one-off efforts permeate the team, and the team is nothing more than a façade.

The Beatles stopped communicating because they began to have trust issues.

As Stephen Covey says, trust has two components—character and competency. Trusting that an individual team member won't deliberately harm another is the character piece. Trusting that a team member won't accidentally harm another is the competency piece. Trust is the foundation of all relationships. Open communication, essential to collaboration, is built upon trust. If a team's trust is violated, getting things done effectively and efficiently becomes difficult to impossible.

The Beatles didn't break up because of competency. They broke up because despite their mega-success, they stopped trusting one another. Teams can put up with a lack of trust for a while and still get the work done. However, as trust erodes, the magic is lost. What the Beatles had in the beginning was pure magic, but as time passed, the complications from a lack of trust—not Yoko Ono—destroyed one of the most influential cultural icons of modern history.

When a team isn't working, drastic measures are sometimes required. When trust is gone and a team is no longer working constructively, the course of action often becomes destructive—and a team needs an intervention.

If the leadership realizes there's a problem and wants to do something about it, but isn't willing to admit just how bad things have gotten, there's a simple trust exercise that demonstrates where things stand between team members.

9.3

TRUST INTERVENTION: NOT FOR THE FAINT OF HEART

The following exercise works best when an outside facilitator conducts it. Here's how it works:

The facilitator gives each team member a bucket with his or her name on it. He or she then gives each team member a marker and the same number of blank cards as there are team members—for example, 16 cards for 16 team members.

The facilitator asks team members to place their labeled buckets around the room. Then, team members rate their trust for the rest of the team members by writing a number between zero and 10 on each card and placing a card in each other team member's bucket. Zero means no trust whatsoever, and 10 means complete trust.

If a team member turns over his or her bucket and it's full of zeros, ones and twos, rehabilitating that person into a functioning member of that team is a challenge. Once trust has been violated, it's hard to get it back.

9.4 Competency versus character

Though the definition of trust may vary from one person to the next, almost everyone has the same definition as to what violates trust. Somewhere in each team member's mental and emotional framework around trust, each has placed certain markers—characteristics of what is a violation of our trust. When that violation occurs, the solution requires more than words. People can behave their way into something that they can't talk their way out of.

Sometimes little things add up to destroy trust. A team member is consistently late to meetings. A team member rarely turns a report in on time. A team member doesn't return calls.

If all components of trust are missing, collaboration can't happen.

If a team is made up of wildly capable, competent people, even if they doubt the character of one another, the work will still get done. It may be painful and inefficient, but the work will get done. Basically, team members say, "I am trusting your competency and not your character." Unfortunately, a common mistake occurs when teams trust character over competency—and it happens all the time.

A team can teach competency, but

> ❝The secret is to gang up on the problem, rather than each other.❞
> – Thomas Stallkamp

character is hard to teach—team members have it or they don't. However, competency versus character is not an either/or proposition. Plenty of teams operate with team members who are trustworthy in both fields. Of course, those are the most successful teams.

The bottom line is finding the right people to be on a team. Without competent people, a team won't succeed in business. Without people of character, a team will waste time, energy and resources. Success may come, but the team won't last.

9.5 Do's and don'ts of team communication

Don't fake it. Insincerity is easy to recognize. It's no coincidence that the first three letters of truth and trust are the same. Insincerity rears its ugly head on both sides of communication—as a speaker and a listener.

Speaking the truth is as much a matter of getting real with oneself as it is about getting real with others. Without sincere words, genuine communication and collaboration simply will not happen.

On the flip side of earnest speech is genuine listening. Becoming a more sincere listener is often just a matter of unselfishly focusing one's thoughts on someone else and the act of listening. Changing the way we think about listening versus having a conversation makes us better listeners.

Listening is about the other person.

Granted, if a team member drones on and on and on repeating the same information or offering little in terms of information and insight, that's something else. That behavior warrants interjecting. However, finding one's way to sincere listening that goes beyond recognizing to becoming genuinely interested in other team members' unique perspectives will take a team a long way toward great communication—and ultimately collaboration.

For those who struggle with listening, here are some pointers:

- Focus. Stop with the multi-tasking. If you're doing something else, you're not listening.
- Even if you disagree, let the speaker finish.
- Make consistent eye contact.
- When appropriate, repeat what was said or encouraging verbal or non-verbal feedback.
- Don't plan a counter-argument while the other person is talking. Just keep listening.
- When the speaker is done, ask questions for clarification.

Try for more face-to-face communication—or have a conversation.

Is it really necessary to schedule practically every phone conversation? No, it's not. Make an effort to have more conversations instead of emailing someone with a simple question. An organization may even consider email free Wednesdays—or something along those lines to shake up (and open up) communication lines.

Demonstrate respect for team members. Genuine respect in interacting with other team members goes a long way. Respect deadlines. Respect other people's time and work. Be on time for meetings. End on time. Be generally courteous and mannerly.

Do something else. When team communication is on the rocks, make an investment in your team. Take time to fly a kite or climb a rock wall or complete a community service project. The return on your investment is likely to be tenfold and may re-open some communication channels that have been frozen for a while.

Be clear on the response that's needed. If an immediate response is needed, let team members know. For example, one manager developed a simple email protocol that conveyed the necessary response in a single word header:

Subject: **Customer**	A customer needs something
Subject: **FYI**	For your information, not urgent
Subject: **Help!**	Need your help
Subject: **Fire!**	Emergency

> **66 Coming together is a beginning; keeping together is progress; working together is success. 99**
> – Henry Ford

9.6 The value of feedback

Giving constructive feedback is about saying something in a way that allows the receiver to keep his or her dignity. Webster defines dignity as the quality or state of being worthy, honored or esteemed. People are more productive and accomplish more when they feel worthy. Offering feedback in a way that shows disrespect or takes away dignity ultimately destroys trust and ultimately breaks apart a team.

Receiving constructive feedback well takes practice. The key is in not getting defensive. Good newspaper editors have often mastered the art of receiving constructive (and sometimes not-so constructive feedback). Like media editors across the country, *El Paso Times* editor Bob Moore once sat in front of a community group and was hammered by a series of citizens concerned about the newspaper's coverage. With each comment, Moore listened carefully. Before he asked for more information, he usually shook his head and said some version of, "You know what, you're right. We didn't do a great job of that."

He then went on to ask for more information or clarification and then explained why the newspaper made the decisions it did. Even on stories that he had written or been a part of, Moore agreed that the paper could have done better. His calm demeanor, attitude and efforts to give the citizens the opportunity to be heard, defused much of the negativity and left the newspaper in a better light with its readers.

The best constructive feedback doesn't veer into personal preferences and stays focused on the issue. It also provides encouragement, support, suggestions on corrective measures and direction.

For most people, if someone delivers feedback poorly, the result is the feedback is received as an insult and ignites other issues or problems.

In the forming of a true collaboration, trust is critical. How team leaders and team members handle feedback relates back to trust. Some team leaders have a tendency to think they'll be perceived as weak if they seek input from their team. However, the best team leaders model behaviors that create successful teams—and one of the most basic tenets of teamwork is the ability and willingness to give and receive feedback. Part of creating constructive feedback is the courage to give it, and part of it is the courage to receive it.

9.7 Feedback provides guardrails

Feedback provides guardrails—it helps to keep team members on the right path. Without it, individual team members and the team as a whole struggle to get to where they're going.

While sharing feedback, there's a fine line between authentic and contrived. Remember that people almost always recognize a lack of sincerity. Choose when to offer sensitive feedback. The challenge lies in the fact that sometimes planned feedback comes across as insincere feedback.

Leadership helps set the stage for how feedback works. If a leader declares that feedback is important, then a group understands the expectation. The biggest way to drive collaboration and feedback is to role model it. If a leader offers it in a way that's respectful of the person and their time, it's positive. The team leader has to be able to listen and not make excuses when faced with negative criticism.

Feedback can—and should—be offered both formally and informally. Whether it's regular round table style meetings, one-on-one team member/team leader meetings, informal phone calls or emails, the company's intranet, internal newsletters, old-fashioned coffee room bulletin boards—whatever works.

For a team to collaborate successfully, team leaders must create informal and formal opportunities for team members to give and receive feedback. Biannual reviews of how a team's feedback opportunities are working are important.

TAKE THE FEEDBACK QUIZ

Read each statement and rate your answers on a scale of 1 to 5. Once you've finished, add the total of each column to get your feedback score. Continue reading to find your profile and consider ways you could improve.

As a receiver of feedback:

(1) (2) (3) (4) (5)   I accept and consider the feedback rather than immediately discarding it.

(1) (2) (3) (4) (5)   I thank the speaker for being frank and trusting.

(1) (2) (3) (4) (5)   I monitor and try to manage how I'm feeling.

(1) (2) (3) (4) (5)   I ask the speaker what I might do differently.

(1) (2) (3) (4) (5)   I seek feedback from others to compare notes.

(1) (2) (3) (4) (5)   I reflect on how to alter my approach in the future.

(1) (2) (3) (4) (5)   I immediately begin to practice a new approach.

(1) (2) (3) (4) (5)   I monitor myself and ask for further feedback.

(1) (2) (3) (4) (5)   I ask for coaching from a mentor.

(1) (2) (3) (4) (5)   I keep the feedback in perspective and don't allow it to destroy my confidence in other areas.

Total: [ ]

1 I never do this

2 I did this once and it didn't work

3 I do this and get mixed results

4 I do this, but I know I could improve

5 I do this all the time

As a giver of feedback:

(1)(2)(3)(4)(5) I start with the positive first.

(1)(2)(3)(4)(5) I think carefully before offering feedback.

(1)(2)(3)(4)(5) Informally, I encourage the other person to tell me how they think things went.

(1)(2)(3)(4)(5) I share details to show that I was paying attention.

(1)(2)(3)(4)(5) I keep feedback short and focused.

(1)(2)(3)(4)(5) I ask questions to make sure my feedback is received as I intended— to build respect, credibility and demonstrate that I care.

(1)(2)(3)(4)(5) I clarify information and adjust my approach when the person is defensive or gives excuses.

(1)(2)(3)(4)(5) I offer feedback only on actions I've witnessed firsthand.

(1)(2)(3)(4)(5) I am consistent with the feedback I offer and do my best to keep subconscious biases in check.

(1)(2)(3)(4)(5) I encourage and get the other person to come up with the next steps.

Total: [ ]

YOUR SCORE SAYS:

If your Feedback Score is 45 or less, you're a **Feedback Novice.**

You've come to the right place. Becoming aware of your shortcomings is the first step. Re-read the 20 statements in the quiz. Which of those could you start practicing today? Make a point to try it by the end of the day—and again tomorrow. Give it a go and see what a difference it makes.

Forming a habit takes three weeks. Improving your ability to give and receive feedback truly could be transformative for you personally and professionally. Take a few minutes and develop a plan to focus on the feedback skills outlined in each of the 20 statements above. Perhaps you might focus on developing or improving one skill for a week at a time.

Depending on your schedule, find a time each week—perhaps Sunday night before the work week starts—to evaluate how the skill is coming along. Find someone who can help keep you accountable. Make a plan of action for the coming week on ways to improve or on developing a new feedback skill. What do you have to lose?

If your Feedback Score is between 46 and 65, you're a **Feedback Apprentice.**

You're on the right track. You're thinking about the feedback you're offering and receiving even though it may not come naturally to you in every situation. You've taken the most difficult steps in the feedback process, now you're ready to take it up another notch.

Review your scores on the 20 feedback statements. Which are your two or three weakest areas? How could you improve on those skills and tactics? Develop an action plan toward mastering your identified concerns. Consider partnering with someone to keep you accountable in your efforts to improve your feedback status.

If your Feedback Score is between 66 and 85, you're a **Feedback Journeyman.**

You are a feedback veteran. Chances are that you're so accustomed to giving and receiving feedback, that you don't even have to think about it anymore. Clearly, you work to inspire those around you.

You're also aware enough to realize that you could be doing better in the feedback department. You have a pretty good idea of what giving good feedback looks like, and you do it most of the time. You also know how to take constructive criticism in a healthy manner. When you slip up, you recognize your mistakes and are working to make those happen less and less. Since you're clearly making an effort, take a look at the feedback statements and determine your strengths and weaknesses. How could you improve? Develop an action plan. Keep up the good work. You're on your way.

If your Feedback Score is between 86 and 100, you're a **Feedback Master.**

You know all about inspiring people around you. You do it on a regular basis. At this point in life, feedback comes naturally to you. You work to give and receive feedback on a daily basis. You've recognized its value and the positive chain of reinforcement it offers you and the people around you.

People trust you. They find you sincere and want to be around you. They recognize that you are used to being a part of good things. They respect you and what you have to say because of your credibility. You are a true leader. Of course, even for you, things don't work out every single time. When that happens, you know how to take a step back and evaluate what happened as well as people's verbal and non-verbal cues and clues. You develop a plan to improve the course of action.

You're one who spends time focusing on your strengths and weaknesses. Keep it up and keep it real. Remember to be honest with yourself. Don't give yourself a break just because you know the right thing to do. You've still got to do it. Make it a point to take time each week to make sure that's what you're really doing. With your skill set and strengths, you are fantastic mentor material. Offering a hand to those on their way up is a part of the circle of things, but you know that, don't you?

9.10

HOW DO YOU CHALLENGE A TEAMMATE?

Challenging a teammate in a way that doesn't create further friction takes practice. Some of these ideas may help:

- Stay away from opinions—base it on facts and argue the facts.

- Stay away from language like 'believe'.

- Don't argue principle or beliefs. No one wins. Everyone loses.

- Don't let the conversation get personal.

- If you're going to challenge principles or belief, convert it to a challenge of fact.

- If you're going to challenge a teammate, assume some level of accountability.

- Validate your accountability—if any—in the discussion.

- Ensure that the body of evidence is thorough and accurate.

- If it's a fact issue, agree on what information would allow the people involved to reach resolution.

- Align and clarify before you challenge.

- Instead of casting judgment, say, "I don't know what you mean by that."

- Find a way to align expectations in the conversation.

- Agree on the definition of the problem that needs to be solved.

9.11 Creating trust accounts

Building trust and collaboration is similar to using Stephen Covey's metaphor of an emotional bank account with others—in personal and professional relationships. Every action and every word either adds or takes away from our trust accounts—which are sometimes called emotional bank accounts.

Every time one person invests in another person, he or she is gaining the respectful appreciation of the other, like investing money in a bank. As time passes, the two people gain more and more understanding and knowledge as to what the other enjoys.

Over time, one person will disappoint the other, but the relationship will continue if the emotional account is built up high enough. Setbacks will fall away and the two will continue to build their relationship on trust and understanding.

9.12 Clarifying roles and responsibilities

On a team, the clarification of roles, rights and responsibilities eliminates confusion and increases collaboration. Common sense makes it clear that if everyone knows what they're supposed to be doing and who's deciding what, work isn't duplicated and gets done more efficiently.

When a team is struggling and confused with "Who does what?" and "Who makes which decision?", the time is right to evaluate roles, rights and responsibilities—and there are a number of tools to use to delineate that. (see Chapters 3, 4 and 5)

NOTES:

> **"I love argument. I love debate. I don't expect anyone to just sit there and agree with me. That's not their job."**
>
> – **Margaret Thatcher**

Summary
Chapter 9: Consistent Communication

1. **Open expression.** Team members are encouraged to express themselves openly and honestly. Who does what. Team members are able to declare what each does for the team.

2. **Feedback.** Team members seek input and constructive feedback from each other on their performance.

3. **Taking responsibility.** Each team member accepts responsibility for getting the work done.

4. **Mastery.** Each team member does his or her job with excellence.

5. **Encouraging dissent.** Team members challenge each other about plans and approaches.

6. **Intent.** Team members trust one another's motives and commitment.

7. **Character.** Team members trust each other not to intentionally harm the team.

8. **Staying informed.** Team members create, share and receive regular progress updates both within and outside the team.

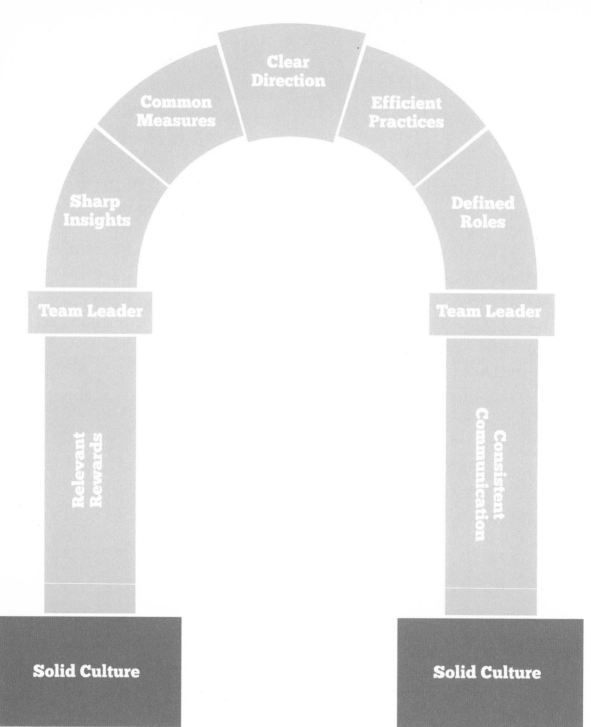

> **Be kind whenever possible. It is always possible.**
> – Dalai Lama

Solid Culture

For a couple of years, back in the 1990s, there was a joke that went something like this:

Los Angeles has a sports team for every fan. If you like hockey, you've got the Ducks. If you like baseball, you've got the Dodgers. If you like football, you've got the Rams. If you like basketball, you've got the Lakers. And, if you don't like basketball, you've got the Clippers.

Though things were looking up after their rousing 2011-2012 season, up until then, the poor beleaguered Los Angeles Clippers had only enjoyed two winning seasons in 30 years. The Clippers have had a culture of losing longer than the New Orleans Saints did. With only seven winning records scattered throughout the 42-year-history of the franchise, getting a good thing going has been hard to come by. No doubt, the Clippers faithful are hoping their more-than-mediocre 2012 finish in the playoffs will be the start of something positive.

In contrast to the Clippers, the Los Angeles Lakers have the NBA's all-time record for number of wins. They have the highest all-time winning percentage. They have appeared in the NBA Finals more than any other team. Having that many wins for that long takes more than stars aligning. The Los Angeles Lakers have a winning culture.

Figuring out what creates the two teams' different cultures is complicated, but eliminating the venue as the deciding factor is easy. Both teams play in the same arena, The Staples Center. Because the Clippers' coaching staff has changed more than a dozen times since 1981, most people lay the blame for the Clippers' woes at the feet of its only constant since 1981—its owner, Donald Sterling.

Sterling's reputation is anything but.

He's widely considered to be a cheapskate. For years, the Los Angeles Clippers practiced in a suburban health club in El Segundo. Finally, in 2008, Sterling built the team a practice facility.

After they moved into The Staples Center for the 1999-2000 season, the team began to build something positive. Their upswing culminated with winning 47 games in the 2005-2006 season. Signing Elton Brand in 2003, for the biggest contract in the Clippers' history—an $82 million six-year deal, played a role in the team's almost-change of fortune, but alas, it fizzled.

More recently, the Clippers' loyal few have renewed hope in dunkmaster and game-changing forward, Blake Griffin. Because of a knee injury, Griffin had to sit out the first season after he was drafted to the Clippers. Healthy and able to play in 2010-2011, the Clippers had great hope that Griffin could help turn the team around. But after his first season, the team finished with a 32-50 record—more than twice as many losses as wins. And after another season, the tide still didn't turn.

Sterling's reputation doesn't end with his legendary frugality.

He has also publicly heckled his own players. Plus, numerous racism accusations haven't helped much either. In 2009, the U.S. Department of Justice sued Sterling for housing discrimination. The case alleged that Sterling refused to rent to non-Koreans in some of his apartments in Los Angeles' Koreatown. The government's lawsuit made bold accusations against Sterling, alleging that he once said he didn't want to rent to Hispanics or African Americans for reasons too despicable to repeat.

> **"In different parts of Africa, wherever chimps have been studied, there are completely different tool-using behaviors. And because it seems that these patterns are passed from one generation to the next, through observation, imitation and practice— that is a definition of human culture."**
>
> – Jane Goodall

But wait, there's more.

In 2004, the Clippers assistant coach Kim Hughes was diagnosed with prostate cancer.

Clippers management denied payment for the $70,000 procedure required to remove the cancer saying, "If we did it for one person, we'd have to do it for everyone." The denial prompted one sportswriter to call Sterling, "the worst person in the world." Fortunately, several of Hughes' players chipped in to pay for the life-saving surgery.

There's even more. There are sexual harassment charges galore. There's the repeatedly touted (by Sterling) but yet to appear $50 million pledge to build a center to provide services to Los Angeles' homeless population.

At some point, regardless of the truth to so many of the allegations against Sterling, the damage is done and practically irreversible. All in all, the owner of the Los Angeles Clippers has a lot of bad juju. The link between the head of an organization and the organization's losing culture is not difficult to discern.

But there is always hope. Time will tell. Changing a culture takes time and effort. If the Clippers organization finally gets the right players and coaches on board, the team itself can play a bigger role in culture—and change the way the organization operates.

However, the leader of an organization should be a role model the rest of the organization can aspire to follow. Aspirational leaders help transform cultures.

10.2 Defining culture

organizational culture: *n.* **The shared values and behaviors that contribute to the unique social and psychological environment of an organization—the personality of the place.**

Actions that are observed in the organization that produce positive and/or negative results are passed on through stories throughout the organization. Those stories teach what success looks like in an organization. The challenge is that the people passing on the stories are usually unaware of some of the implications created by the norm the stories set.

For example, an executive may laud Larry, the employee who stayed up all night long to prepare for a presentation. Larry's actions are deemed an example of his can-do-get-it-done attitude rather than leading to questions about Larry's time-management skills, procrastination and lack of focus—all of which could be reasons why Larry had to stay up all night. So when Larry is praised for working through the night, Larry's lack of organization and time-management issues are rewarded, and those watching may choose to emulate.

Behaviors in the workplace lead to a company's culture and the developed competencies influence the behaviors. The competencies are how we get work done. The ease in which work gets completed leads to more positive cultural elements—less stress, more respect, more civility and just general happiness.

To gain insights to an organization's culture, consider the answers that your company would give to the following questions:

- **How are customer relationships viewed?**
- **How is success defined?**
- **How are people rewarded for performance?**
- **How are decisions made?**
- **What types of people does the organization attract?**
- **What types of people does the organization promote?**
- **How is conflict resolved?**

> **" In a controversy, the instant we feel anger we have already ceased striving for the truth, and have begun striving for ourselves. "**
>
> – Buddha

Most companies have stated cultures they want to portray—and they use a variety of means to do so, from break room posters to engraved stones in the lobby. However, they also have a set of stories that define the culture better than pocket mantras and posters. The stories that support the answers reveal the company's actual culture.

10.3 Elements that make up culture

Anyone who has ever been a part of an organization that decided to try to change its culture knows the difficulties that line the path of the effort. However, in some instances, change is necessary for survival. When leaders recognize the need for a shift in organizational culture, they must first define and delineate its culture.

Defining a culture can be difficult. Most people simply consider culture as "the way we do things around here."

Astute team members recognize the subtle and not-so-subtle unwritten characteristics of an organization's culture and adapt them as principles and standards to work by. If unproductive elements of culture exist, most new hires are quickly indoctrinated—even the ones who need help in deciphering the unwritten ways of an organization.

If an organization is doing its best to focus on certain areas of change, incorporating new hire orientations, training programs and mentoring programs that focus on the areas of change are beneficial to helping employees become accustomed to the ways and means of an organization.

When people want to understand a specific business or organization, they must also understand the basic elements of organizational culture and the relationship between culture and performance.

10.4 PINPOINTING WEAKNESSES & EVALUATING CULTURE:

1. There is a lack of trust.
2. There is poor overall performance.
3. Collaboration is not prevalent.
4. There is a lack of clear purpose or direction.
5. Decision-making is either slow and/or inaccurate.
6. Esprit de corps is weak.

Some examples of questions to ask to further understand an organization's culture and of how it affects organizational performance follow:

Group norms, habits and observed behaviors: For example, is it acceptable to start meetings late and does the organization have a problem meeting deadlines?

Values statement: Is there a disconnect between the organization's formal values statement and reality?

Climate: Is there an atmosphere of fear and hostility or generosity and benevolence?

Myths and metaphors: Do organizational legends include wild extravagances at the executive level while those down in the trenches are buying their own paper clips and note pads?

Rituals: Are significant individual or team contributions celebrated with flair?

Accumulated shared learning/history: Does the organization have a history of being the underdog and working to topple a major competitor?

Symbols: Does every executive in the company have their own covered garage while everyone else parks in the rain?

Career ladder: Does the organization promote the best candidates or the favored candidates?

Noise: Whose voice is heard?

Rewards: Is the organization rewarding the behavior it's looking for or just the opposite?

10.5 My name is Joe...and I have a problem

Like a good 12-step program, the first step toward changing something is admitting there's a problem. Changing an organization's culture begins the same way. Both the brilliance and problem of a team are the people. There comes a time when organizational leaders have to realize and admit that what they are doing—and what is happening within the organization—is not working. As with so many issues, awareness is the single biggest issue. So, how can an organization change its culture?

Resolving problems requires that team members come to alignment and agreement that they have to develop a new way of doing things, which means:

- They have to identify what's not working.
- They have to clarify their values.
- They have to put some tracking mechanisms in place and gather data.
- Using the information gleaned, the team evaluates the results it's getting and the results it seeks.

They also have to ask lots of questions:

- Are the results meeting expectations? If not, why not?
- What are the top five issues?
- Is it a product issue? If so, specifically what element?
- Is it a customer issue? If so, what is the specific issue?
- Is it a competition issue? If so, what is the specific issue?
- Is it a channel issue? If so, what is the specific issue?
- Is there a problem with a specific process?
- Does the bigger issue go back to a problem with one specific leadership trait?
- Are expectations realistic?

Examining past errors and making amends can lead to learning to work in a different way with different behaviors—which leads to a different culture.

EVALUATING YOUR ORGANIZATIONAL CULTURE

Without an alteration of the fundamental goals, values and expectations of organizations or individuals, change remains superficial and short-term. Even if the bottom line offers a telltale sign that an organization's culture needs tweaking.

If the team isn't getting the results it needs, it's time to evaluate the culture. Often the results are behavior driven. Often, the creative or competitive or collaborative nature of a team doesn't allow its members to behave differently to produce different results. If team members are disengaged and not rallying around the team, it is not always a reflection of their interest but is often connected to the culture of the team. Teams take time. They take investment and energy.

Where does your organizational culture fit?

COMMANDING   **VISIONARY**   **COOPERATIVE**   **ENTERPRISING**

WANT A MORE COMMANDING CULTURE?

Leadership Style:
directive, numbers-based, organized

The Team:
power, authority, heirarchal influence

The Results:
is smooth-running, is methodical, has low margin of error, meets commitments, has dependable delivery

- Formalize structures
- Set clear policies and procedures
- Create more documentation
- Set verification processes

WANT A MORE VISIONARY CULTURE?

Leadership Style:
creative, leading edge, innovative

The Team:
individualists, mavericks

The Results:
pushes the envelope, acquires new learning, is proactive versus reactive, created new products and/or services, promotes calculated risks

- Hire people who are proven innovators
- Encourage risk taking
- Don't punish failure; learn from it
- Be flexible
- Create an open physical work environment
- Demonstrate a commitment to experimentation and innovation

WANT A MORE COOPERATIVE CULTURE?

Leadership Style:
teacher, mentor

The Team:
motivated, engaging

The Results:
strong teamwork, more alignment, a friendlier place to work, improved morale, more consensus, collective problem-solving

- Teach team problem solving
- Introduce team rewards
- Include peer collaboration measures in the performance review process
- Teach teamwork skills
- Promote team players, not just individual contributors
- Add collaborative physical space in the work environment
- Create a mentoring program
- Create non-working opportunities for team members to get to know each other
- Strive for a friendlier atmosphere in the office

WANT A MORE ENTERPRISING CULTURE?

Leadership Style:
results-driven, competitive, market-focused

The Team:
high achievers, type A personalities

The Results:
focuses on goals and targets, creates hard-driving competition within the organization, centers on winning, culls weak performance

- Focus on and reward results
- Set clear goals and expectations
- Create literal competitions to reach goals
- Hire leaders who are proven hard-driving, tough competitors
- Make transparent various team performance factors

10.7 Say you want to change your culture?

To create change, an organization has to address and navigate the barriers of speed, conflict and civility.

NOTES:

10.8
SIX STEPS TO INSTILL A SENSE OF URGENCY AND SPEED IN TEAMS:

Speed and a sense of urgency are set by a team's direction and the measures that are in place. Measures lead a team to speed—or not. Time is important, and teams need regular reminders that they're operating on deadline. A six-month objective will put significantly more pressure on the team than an 18-month objective. Simply put, if leaders put tighter measures and rewards in place—with clear time elements, a team's sense of urgency increases. In order to increase an organization's sense of speed, try the following ideas and pointers:

1. Share the vision of why change is needed in the time that it is needed. Do not expect people to know why change is important or to agree with your assessment of the timing required. Share the vision. Make it simple. Then, they will be able to see and agree with you on the urgency.

2. Make your team a key part of winning. People will move forward faster if they think they will have a "win" on the other end and some kind of benefit out of it. Winning requires a clear picture of the goal and the means to the end. If the team needs coaching, do it! If they need tools, give them the tools. Set the expectation that your team is doing the work to win and accomplish a key goal.

3. Train team members so they know how to work together and so that when they do, they work better. You don't take an unproven team into battle and expect great speed—its members haven't worked together and haven't perfected the collaborative environment. Set realistic expectations for your team and then allow the team to demonstrate the skills everyone has learned.

4. Show your team, by example, what winning looks like and then challenge them to follow your lead. Nothing makes people better than a winning leader. That demonstration is not only to show off (though there is some good in showing a competitive spirit), but to show them how to get the work done. Teams and team leaders can't be afraid of high performance. If one person is better than the rest, give that person the opportunity not only to "show off," but to "show how."

5. Allow some healthy internal competition. The right balance builds a healthy competitive spirit in the team. It also removes the tendency for people to develop "groupthink" where no one challenges team members to move fast or do better. Groupthink can set in like arthritis in an athlete. Teams often need permission to break passivity.

6. Celebrate examples of winning and speed. If speed is one of the cultural elements of the company or team, sharing and promoting examples of winning speed adds value. Many people say that speed and accuracy do not go together, but a look at a professional tennis match disproves that line of thought. Speed and accuracy align when there is discipline and practice.

10.9 Managing conflict

conflict: *n.* **A fight or a war; sharp disagreement as of interest or ideas; emotional disturbance.**

Conflict is a necessary condition of social interaction—even though families, churches and schools often teach that conflict is bad and should be avoided. Yes, unproductive conflict should be avoided. Unproductive conflict destroys relationships. It results from bad decisions and uses a team's energy for nonproductive ends. However, productive conflicts can fuel growth and learning. If disagreements are directed towards a positive end, people feel respected and relationships are maintained.

Conflict is indicative of a bigger problem. Managing conflict is about moving the issue from the subjective to the objective. The interaction between the two parties becomes less about the issue and more about achieving the goal. If two people become aligned to the outcome, conflict can be managed effectively.

A lot of times, conflict is either based in misaligned values or misaligned facts.

For conflict to come to a positive resolution, the people involved have to find their common interests. However, a conflict of values can seldom be fully solved.

When conflict occurs, if the sticking point comes down to one person believing that he or she can't work through a trust issue using words, then it's time to enact the old adage, "Actions speak louder than words." However, if a team member simply doesn't trust another's character, and the conflict is based on trust, the conflict is not going to be fixed.

10.10 Civility in the workplace

Leaders must establish operating principals that emphasize the importance of respectfulness and civility. Then, those leaders need to enact a zero-tolerance for disrespectful engagements or even language.

For example, if someone makes fun of another person and the leader doesn't shut it down, then he or she is propagating the behavior. One of the elements that make a team work is standing up for the team's values. In a respectful culture, one team member is not going to talk negatively about other individuals without someone raising their hand and saying, "That's not a good conversation."

Civility in the workplace allows individuals to work better together and can assist in the process of team members becoming aligned with the culture of a company. There are two types of basic values—the negotiable and the non-negotiable.

Teams and organizations need to define both types of values and set priorities around them.

People need to act in accordance with the established values of the organization as a condition of their continued employment. There is some shared responsibility for establishing values, but the shared responsibility does not imply a company is a democracy.

Everyone defines values differently as well, so no matter what the those values are, they must be defined in terms of behaviors (things people can see) so that team members have clear expectations and can hold one another accountable.

10.11 Rules of Civility

As a schoolboy, at some point before he turned 16 years old, George Washington had copied out in longhand 110 rules of behavior, based on a set of rules composed by French Jesuits in 1595. Many believe one of the reasons George Washington was able to lead effectively was the respect he garnered from almost everyone, regardless of their social standing. Mason Locke Weems, who wrote *The Life of Washington* way back in 1800, wrote the fable of George Washington chopping down the cherry tree. Weems also wrote that it was "no wonder every body honoured him who honoured every body."

Richard Brookhiser, a journalist and historian, wrote, "Washington was to dedicate himself to freeing America from a court's control. Could manners survive the operation? Without realizing it, the Jesuits who wrote them, and the young man who copied them, were outlining and absorbing a system of courtesy appropriate to equals and near-equals."

The Jesuit written-George Washington-imparted rules are good reminders for today's society. Though some are surely dated, most of the rules are as timely now as they were in 1595. In language of long ago that's worth figuring out, what follows is a sampling, complete with Washington's spelling and syntax of yore:

From
The Rules of Civility
as written by George Washington

Based on a set of rules composed by French Jesuits in 1595

1st

Every Action done in Company, ought to be with Some Sign of Respect, to those that are Present.

2d

When in Company, put not your Hands to any Part of the Body, not usualy Discovered.

14th

Turn not your Back to others especially in Speaking, Jog not the Table or Desk on which Another reads or writes, lean not upon any one.

17th

Be no Flatterer, neither Play with any that delights not to be Play'd Withal.

19th

Let your Countenance be pleasant but in Serious Matters Somewhat grave.

22d

Shew not yourself glad at the Misfortune of another though he were your enemy.

24th

Do not laugh too loud or too much at any Publick Spectacle.

35th
Let your Discourse with Men of Business be Short and Comprehensive.

41st
Undertake not to Teach your equal in the art himself Proffesses; it Savours of arrogancy.

42d
Let thy ceremonies in Courtesie be proper to the Dignity of his place with whom thou conversest for it is absurd to act the same with a Clown and a Prince.

44th
When a man does all he can though it Succeeds not well blame not him that did it.

47th
Mock not nor Jest at any thing of Importance break no Jest that are Sharp Biting and if you Deliver any thing witty and Pleasent abstain from Laughing there at yourself.

49th
Use no Reproachfull Language against any one neither Curse nor Revile.

50th
Be not hasty to believe flying Reports to the Disparagement of any.

54th
Play not the Peacock, looking every where about you, to See if you be well Deck't, if your Shoes fit well if your Stokings sit neatly, and Cloths handsomely.

56th
Associate yourself with Men of good Quality if you Esteem your own Reputation; for 'tis better to be alone than in bad Company.

59th
Never express anything unbecoming, nor Act agst the Rules Moral before your inferiours.

60th
Be not immodest in urging your Friends to Discover a Secret.

62d

Speak not of doleful Things in a Time of Mirth or at the Table; Speak not of Melancholy Things as Death and Wounds, and if others Mention them Change if you can the Discourse tell not your Dreams, but to your intimate Friend.

63d

A Man ought not to value himself of his Atchievements, or rare Qualities of wit; much less of his riches Virtue or Kindred.

72d

Speak not in an unknown Tongue in Company but in your own Language and that as those of Quality do and not as the Vulgar; Sublime matters treat Seriously.

73d

Think before you Speak pronounce not imperfectly nor bring out your Words too hastily but orderly & distinctly.

77th

Treat with men at fit Times about Business & Whisper not in the Company of Others.

78th

Make no Comparisons and if any of the Company be Commended for any brave act of Vertue, commend not another for the Same.

79th

Be not apt to relate News if you know not the truth thereof. In Discoursing of things you Have heard Name not your Author always A Secret Discover not.

81st

Be not Curious to Know the Affairs of Others neither approach those that Speak in Private.

82d

Undertake not what you cannot perform but be carefull to keep your promise.

89th

Speak not Evil of the absent for it is unjust.

91st

Make no Shew of taking great Delight in
your Victuals, Feed not with Greediness; cut
your Bread with a Knife, lean not
on the Table neither find fault with what
you Eat.

92d

Take no Salt or cut Bread
with your Knife Greasy.

99th

Drink not too leisurely nor yet too hastily.
Before and after Drinking wipe your Lips
breath not then or Ever with too Great a
Noise, for it is uncivil.

105th

Be not Angry at Table
whatever happens & if you have reason
to be so, Shew it not but on a Chearfull
Countenance especially if there be Strangers
for Good Humour makes one
Dish of Meat a Feast.

110th

Labour to keep alive in your Breast that
Little Spark of Celestial fire Called Conscience.

NOTES:

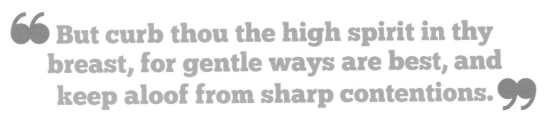

> **" But curb thou the high spirit in thy breast, for gentle ways are best, and keep aloof from sharp contentions. "**
>
> – Homer

10.12 A final word on culture: Diversity

Diversity of thought is critical to high-functioning teams. Incorporating people with different thinking styles, skills, experience, perspective and leadership builds a team's strength.

Using an assessment tool like Myers Briggs or Hermann Brain Dominance Instrument (HBDI) to discover team members' thinking styles is essential to a team struggling with solving a challenge. The assessment tools can assist in finding out what thinking styles are on an existing team. That knowledge can lead the team to realize where the holes are.

10.13 Watch Out

Team members behave themselves into problems—and no one can talk their way out of problems they've behaved themselves into. Behaviors are the only way to earn trust back. As the old adage says, actions speak louder than words. Leaders develop followers, sometimes from unwilling participants, but that is still the challenge, even in the business environment.

> **"When you learn something from people, or from a culture, you accept it as a gift, and it is your lifelong commitment to preserve it and build on it."**
>
> – Yo-Yo Ma

Summary
Chapter 10: Solid Culture

1. **Stating values:** The team has a written set of values that guides behavior.

2. **Living values:** The team walks the talk related to stated values.

3. **Customer focus:** The team focuses on delivering customer expectations, both internal and external.

4. **Rituals:** The team takes the time to celebrate good performance, team transitions and meaningful personal events.

5. **Sense of urgency:** The team considers time to be a critical resource.

6. **Conflict management:** The team manages conflict through open and forthright communication.

7. **Conflict resolution:** The team takes a proactive stance on solving conflict by focusing on the facts versus opinions.

8. **Dignity and respect:** Team members treat one another with respect.

9. **Civility:** The team exhibits conduct that demonstrates courtesy, politeness and civility.

10. **Diversity:** The team's diverse skills, experience and perspectives enhance their ability to work effectively.

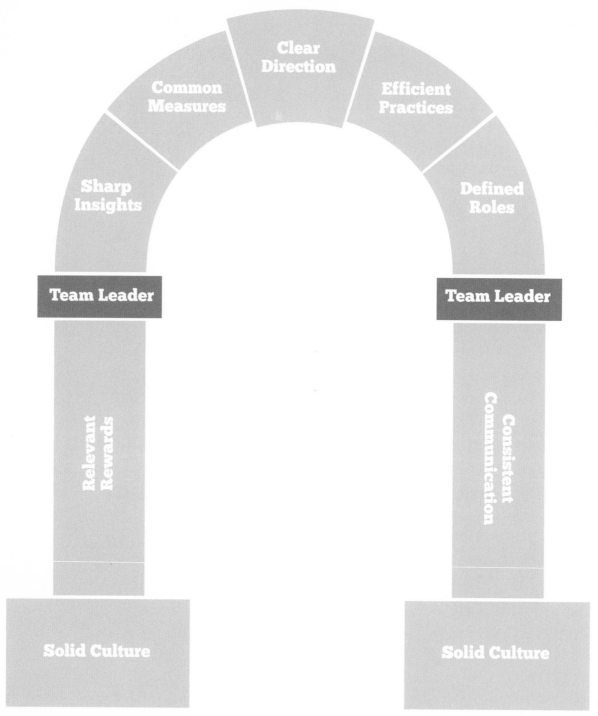

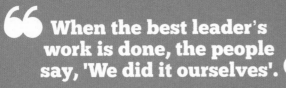

> **"When the best leader's work is done, the people say, 'We did it ourselves'. "**
> — Lao Tzu

Team Leader

Regardless of the field, the value of experience comes in the chance to recognize what works—and what doesn't.

The best leaders find common threads of achievements. They refine and build upon triumphs. They learn from failures. They grow. Building on the old adage, "A wise man learns from the mistakes of others; a fool learns only from his own," a range of leaders shared their wisdom on what works in leading a team.

The leaders, from a variety of industries, range in age from 27 to 61. They have diverse backgrounds—educational, functional and cultural. However, the leaders all share the experience of having successfully led a variety of teams. Each of the dozen leaders was willing to share their expertise and insights on what has worked and what hasn't worked leading teams. The leaders answered four simple questions: 1. What characteristics have the highly successful teams you've led shared? 2. What traits or situations have led teams to struggle? 3. What would you have done differently—both on teams that were successful and on teams that struggled? 4. How important is the role of team leader to the team's success?

Their answers demonstrate the broad range of wisdom, experience and perspective leadership offers. Their answers also support the Team Arch® model. They emphasize the importance of a team knowing, understanding and buying into the "clear direction" it is heading. They recognize the importance of trust. They understand the value of communication and follow-through.

They gave examples that demonstrated that they realize the importance of recognizing, addressing and correcting traits and situations that lead teams down difficult paths.

Clearly these leaders realize that other than backyard baseball, do-overs are hard to come by. However, they appreciated the opportunities along the way to look back and evaluate the what could have beens and what would have beens that could have led to a change of plans going forward.

They also touch on the less tangible stuff that great teams are made of. Though they use different words ranging from team spirit to intimacy to mysticism, nearly all of the leaders interviewed for this project touched on the importance of recognizing the human element of teams.

Also, they were all quick to point out the importance of the whole team. Throughout the interview process, none of these leaders—though they have achieved great things—were know-it-alls. They expressed a curiosity and a willingness to help—to share what might be of service to others. In essence, they demonstrate that leaders who continue to succeed listen, retain sufficient humility and remember whom they serve.

NOTES:

What universal characteristics do highly successful teams share?

> **"Capable people who value each other."**
>
> **Dr. Charlie Skipper**
> *Headmaster, Episcopal School of Acadiana*
> *Lafayette, Louisiana*

> ***"The right talent is not to be under looked—having the right people in the right jobs is critical."***
>
> **Chris Kiser**
> *President of the Brands Division*
> *AdvancePierre Foods, Edmond, Oklahoma*

> "Finding joy in the process. Having fun along the way. Being serious enough to get the job done but not being so serious that it's not fun."
>
> **Jeffrey Schwartz**
> *Co-Founder, The Next One's on Me*
> *Austin, Texas*

> ***"They have high-performing behavior: working calmly through conflict and focused on team success."***
>
> **Bob Landis**
> *Vice president, People and Organization*
> *Mars Chocolate, Mt. Olive, New Jersey*

> "There has to be a truly compelling common objective. I believe it is critical that the common objective be focused on purpose—a purpose not numbers. I don't believe you can run a team focused on numbers. Successful teams focus on the ultimate end of the business. They figure out what their ultimate goal is and then track the things that directly relate to achieving that goal. They ask the question, 'What is the most important thing we can do, right now, to accomplish our objectives?' "
>
> **Lee Rodriguez**
> *Former Procter & Gamble and U.S. Army*
> *San Antonio, Texas*

"They trust each other."

Omar Hoek
*Vice President, Marketing of Food/Medical
Ahlstrom, Lyon, France*

*"Everyone on the team
contributes...no slackers."*

Mark Adkins
*President, San Francisco Chronicle
San Francisco, California*

*"They have a purpose. They
have a reason for being—
that's clearly No. 1."*

Jose Davila
*Vice president, Human Resources
Gap, San Francisco, California*

*"An intimacy—I'm a great believer
in making room for the team to be
creative and connect as individuals."*

Serge Zimmerlin
*Vice President, Human Resources, SGD Group
Paris, France*

"Our most successful teams have a
common vision of where we're trying to
go and how to get there. They ask and can
answer, 'What is the plan for success?'
Respect is absolutely critical—respect
for all individuals and that everyone is
speaking at the team table from a place of
shared vision and success. The voices have
to balance, regardless of where people fit in
the organization. The best teams also have
a fluid understanding of roles and responsibilities. As teams evolve, sometimes roles
shift. There has to be some fluidity."

Michelle Stacy
President, Keurig Inc., Reading, Massachusetts

**What characteristics
do you think successful
teams share?**

_____

_____

_____

_____

*"They have a culture of accepting
feedback–positive and not-so-
positive."*

Katie Ortego Pritchett
*Doctoral candidate at University of Texas in Higher
Education Administration Program, Austin, Texas*

11.3 Learning from failures
What traits or situations lead teams to struggle?

> **"Lack of communication and a disregard for deadlines."**
>
> **Katie Ortego Pritchett**
> *Doctoral candidate at University of Texas in Higher Education Administration Program, Austin, Texas*

> **"The competency of the leader is questioned by the team. The role of the leader is not clear across the group."**
>
> **Chris Kiser**
> *President of the Brands Division AdvancePierre Foods, Edmond, Oklahoma*

'The cheese moves. On one team, we had good people, but the team was not about continual learning—they began to miss things. Over time, in all systems, things change. People change. Skill and knowledge change. The customer changes. Like Alice in *Alice in Wonderland* said,'You have to run faster and faster to stay in the same place.' The team didn't focus on the core processes and continual learning. They were focused on the numbers. They ended up muscling the system. As the system changed and the people changed, the level of alignment within the team went down. Then they got in a spiral—which, in their minds, required more and more muscle. More muscle led to less alignment, fewer relationships, less synergy. The less you have; the less you have. The team's interdependence and their relationships had gone down so far that they began to spiral out of control. They didn't move with the cheese, and the cheese is always moving."

Lee Rodriguez
*Former Procter & Gamble and U.S. Army
San Antonio, Texas*

> **"Too much democracy in the decisions. The team wandered and lost focus."**
>
> **Mark Adkins**
> *President, San Francisco Chronicle*
> *San Francisco, California*

"People not following through. Being pro-active early on is important, but only if you are commited to doing so and will follow through with what you propose."

Jeffrey Schwartz
Co-Founder, The Next One's on Me
Austin, Texas

"The No. 1 thing that causes teams to struggle, in my experience, is when the team lacks not just vision—but also framework. As a group, they have got to be within the ballpark of what they are working toward. The lack of that framework is difficult to overcome. Next, is territoriality—when they're working on their own agendas. The third thing is a lack of a willingness from the group to invest of themselves."

Dr. Charlie Skipper
Headmaster, Episcopal School of Acadiana
Lafayette, Louisiana

"If the team is able to develop a sort of team mysticism—if there's a feeling of, 'We belong to something different and something special'— that ethereal piece will allow the team to do bigger and better things. It's the trickiest element to create, but if you're able to make it happen, it takes the team to a whole different level."

Joao Adao
Vice President, General Manager,
Avery Dennison, Spanish-speaking
South America, Buenos Aries, Argentina

> **"Variable talent capabilities— there were always one or two people who weren't pulling their weight."**
>
> **Bob Landis**
> *Vice president, People and Organization*
> *Mars Chocolate, Mt. Olive, New Jersey*

"Certain members of the team were too positionally strong or personality strong. It was no longer about the team. Instead, it was about the star player."

Michelle Stacy
President, Keurig Inc.
Reading, Massachusetts

'It's hard for a team to self-regulate and move forward when it hasn't had had good leadership. There hasn't been someone to cajole and lead.'

Jose Davila
Vice president, Human Resources
Gap, San Francisco, California

'Ego in team can create some destruction. Not putting forward the general interest, but having an individual putting his or her own agenda before the team agenda.'

Serge Zimmerlin
Vice President, Human Resources
SGD Group, Paris, France

What do you think leads teams to struggle?

_____

_____

_____

_____

_____

In retrospect, what would you have done differently—both on teams that were successful and on teams that struggled?

"I would have taken more time building the team's objectives with each individual's direct and personal involvement. This method will take a bit longer, but the team will be much more effective if it has a strong sense of community and buy-in because everyone's voice is heard. Also, to eliminate surprises, I would have added a step in the formal review process to systematically evaluate and address external changes in the marketplace, since strategy review sessions typically tend to be too internally focused."

Joao Adao
Vice President, General Manager,
Avery Dennison, Spanish-speaking
South America, Buenos Aries, Argentina

"I would have moved quickly to replace non-performers or redefine their role. I would move in and make decisions for the team when the group was indecisive."

Mark Adkins
President, San Francisco Chronicle
San Francisco, California

"Regardless of how it turned out, I usually wish I would have documented the process along the way—who did what, when, how. Then, I could have the data to figure out root causes for both success and failure and what I should have done differently."

Jeffrey Schwartz
Co-Founder, The Next One's on Me
Austin, Texas

> "One of the things I would try to do better is to disengage myself and empower others to act. It's too easy for people to defer to the leadership role."
>
> **Dr. Charlie Skipper**
> *Headmaster, Episcopal School of Acadiana*
> *Lafayette, Louisiana*

> "Good chairmanship and facilitation is half the work."
>
> **Omar Hoek**
> *Vice-President of Marketing of Food/Medical*
> *Ahlstrom, Lyon, France*

> "On the teams that struggled, I would have taken a stronger leadership role in pushing them forward. I personally tend to be deferential to a line leader. There have been times when teams didn't do so well when I should have gotten more involved. On teams that have succeeded, I would celebrate more. When you have an intensive team, you get into a groove and keep working. I don't think you find or take the time to celebrate enough. I believe people appreciate the opportunity to do a little celebrating more than we sometimes realize."
>
> **Jose Davila**
> *Vice president, Human Resources*
> *Gap, San Francisco, California*

Watch Out:

> "Functional expertise does not always make the best team leader."
>
> **Omar Hoek**
> *Vice President, Marketing of Food/Medical*
> *Ahlstrom, Lyon, France*

> "I would have listened more."
>
> **Michelle Stacy**
> *President, Keurig Inc.*
> *Reading, Massachusetts*

"As a leader, what I think I've done wrong is not to be rigorous enough on decisions. Right up front we often see potential issues. You try and coach the team and give them a chance to succeed on their own—but nine times out of ten, we end up doing what we knew from the beginning. Also, we probably don't engage quickly enough with stakeholders. I wish I had checked with stakeholders right up front. As soon as you get clear on stakeholder expectations and align the team to the objectives, it's easier to get a top-notch team to reach high performance."

Bob Landis
Vice President, People and Organization
Mars Chocolate, Mt. Olive, New Jersey

"As I've looked back, I would tell you that first and foremost, I would make sure there's no confusion—no semantics issues on what the objectives are. I want the objectives to be very transparent to all members of the team. There are times when I've taken for granted the clarity was there."

Chris Kiser
President of the Brands Division
AdvancePierre Foods, Edmond, Oklahoma

"Early on, there were times when I noticed individuals who exhibited red flags through their behavior. Often, they were looking to promote individual interests over the group interest. In retrospect, I would have addressed the issues early on."

Katie Ortego Pritchett
Doctoral candidate at University of Texas in Higher Education Administration Program Austin, Texas

Watch Out:

"I'd also be more aware of my ability to impede good things from happening outside of me or around me. It's easier for a leader to be an impediment than a key to success. The leader can kill something a lot more easily than he or she can make it happen."

Dr. Charlie Skipper
Headmaster, Episcopal School of Acadiana, Lafayette, Louisiana

What would you have done differently?

_____

_____

_____

_____

_____

11.5 The importance of leadership

In your opinion, how important is the role of the team leader to the team's success?

'I'm calling it more of a team facilitator. A good leader will engage the team rather than lead the team and take the credit. Good leaders put the success of the team before their own success. Having people challenge ideas, concepts and processes is good, but if it goes too far, it will become toxic and destroy the team. A good team leader has to be willing to make the tough calls on when to remove that person from the team.''

Serge Zimmerlin
Vice President, Human Resources, SGD Group
Paris, France

"On one hand, I think the strength of the team is defined by each individual member's ability to contribute. The more diverse the points of view, the better the outcome will be. From that perspective, the team leader has just another role on the team contributing his opinion, while making sure all the individual opinions are heard. On the other hand, you also need a strong leader who can create that kind of environment where members feel safe enough to communicate their own ideas, can orchestrate that team dynamic effectively and ultimately combine all those ideas into a single, clear, managable plan."

Joao Adao
Vice President, General Manager,
Avery Dennison, Spanish-speaking
South America, Buenos Aries, Argentina

"You need to have a leader—people running around need direction. The role itself is vital. Ultimately someone has to decide right or left up or down."

Jeffrey Schwartz
Co-Founder, The Next One's on Me
Austin, Texas

"On teams when there's been a tough problem, if you don't have a leader who can make a call, you get stuck."

Jose Davila
Vice president, Human Resources
Gap, San Francisco, California

"On the continuum from needing to be led to being self-directed, the ultimate goal of a leader is to get the team to the point that it's self-directed and doesn't need a leader any more. The first part is to ensure that every member of the team is committed and accountable. Ensure all the voices around the table are heard fairly and the team stays in balance."

Michelle Stacy
President, Keurig Inc.,
Reading, Massachusetts

"If you are very successful in your role, you get over-empowered. It's so nice on the ego gratification side, but it's bad leadership—and in the long run, that's bad for an institution. None of us are omniscient. When the problems come, if people are used to working together, they will push through the issues and carry on."

Dr. Charlie Skipper
Headmaster, Episcopal School of Acadiana Lafayette, Louisiana

"The leader may or may not play an important role in a high-performing team. A great leader understands that achieving a high level of performance may mean to get out of the way and listen."

Mark Adkins
President, San Francisco Chronicle San Francisco, California

"It changes. In the beginning, the leader's role is model and catalyst. Someone has to hold up the mirror and say, 'Let me show you a better way.' Over time, the leader becomes more of a coach."

Bob Landis
Vice President, People and OrganizationMars Chocolate, Mt. Olive, New Jersey

"It's everything to a team's success. If a team leader doesn't mirror what the team is trying to achieve, the team doesn't function. Without a high performing leader, it's rare to find a high-performing team."

Chris Kiser
President of the Brands Division AdvancePierre Foods, Edmond, Oklahoma

How important do you think the team leader is to the team's success?

11.6 Additional thoughts on leadership

"Leadership isn't always positional. Sometimes someone comes from the middle of the pack and can motivate the team."

Katie Ortego Pritchett
Doctoral candidate at University of Texas in Higher Education Administration Program, Austin, Texas

"A high-performing team isn't just about the right mix of individual capabilities. It's also about being 'at stake' for each other. When one team member will spontaneously reach beyond the scope of his or her role to help another team member in order to ensure the team succeeds."

Bob Landis
Vice President, People and Organization Mars Chocolate, Mt. Olive, New Jersey

"Leadership and power are kind of like the concept of love. It really boils down to one of those interesting ideas that there's more of it, the more you give away."

Dr. Charlie Skipper
Headmaster, Episcopal School of Acadiana Lafayette, Louisiana

"I think there's something around the team doing self-evaluation and self-monitoring—this idea that you have a way to evaluate your effectiveness. The real sophisticated teams, the ones successful moving forward, they have some metrics to help them move better."

Jose Davila
Vice president, Human Resources Gap, San Francisco, California

"At the end of the day, the leader needs to provide a productive environment and encourage some fun across the team. The ones who drop their boundaries and understand how to work with other people are the most successful."

Omar Hoek
Vice President, Marketing of Food/Medical Ahlstrom, Lyon, France

> "I'm a firm believer that having respect for each other in a social environment is critical to a team's success. My most successful teams have all gone out and done something fun together. The bond that can be created in a non-work environment is absolutely critical to a team's success. It levels the playing field."

Michelle Stacy
President, Keurig Inc., Reading, Massachusetts

> "Do I have the right people on the bus?' Once the leader assembles the right team, his or her role is no more important than any other team member."

Bob Landis
Vice President, People and Organization
Mars Chocolate, Mt. Olive, New Jersey

> "You have to be passionate. In any change effort, and successful teams are constantly about change, there will be difficulties and setbacks. The leader has to be passionate. He's got to believe in the mission and organization more than anyone else. When the going gets tough, he must constantly remind people of the vision and keep the goals in front of everyone. Everything looks like a failure in the middle. The leader has to ensure the team believes in the vision and themselves. There's nothing a small group of people can't accomplish if they believe in the cause and each other."

Lee Rodriguez
Former Proctor & Gamble and U.S. Army
San Antonio, Texas

Watch Out:

"The leader should handle the 10 percent that escalates and can't be solved—and only 10 percent."

Bob Landis
Vice President, People and Organization
Mars Chocolate, Mt. Olive, New Jersey

Additional thoughts on leadership:

_____

_____

_____

_____

_____

_____

_____

_____

_____

_____

_____

_____

_____

_____

_____

_____

"Leadership cannot really be taught. It can only be learned."

— Harold S. Geneen

Summary
Chapter 11: Team Leader

1. **Clear direction:** A team leader ensures that a team is focused on the objective, has common buy-in and understands its shared vision.

2. **Common measures:** A team leader aligns the team to a set of measures that clearly define what success looks like—setting in motion a sense of urgency, accountability and evaluation.

3. **Efficient practices:** A team leader guides the team to develop the plan and operate with practices and processes to deliver the objectives.

4. **Defined roles:** A team leader builds and maintains a team with the right talent, clear in their roles and responsibilities.

5. **Sharp insights:** A team leader creates an environment where teams gather data, create insights and continue learning.

6. **Relevant rewards:** A team leader focuses and motivates the team with the appropriate balance of rewards, recognition and celebration.

7. **Consistent communication:** A team leader makes certain that all team members' voices are heard and that formal and informal lines of communication remain open.

8. **Solid culture:** A team leader builds community based on trust, transparency and shared values.

12

Team Assessment

Is your team getting the job done? Are you working together well? Have you identified the strengths, snags and shortcomings in the way your team works?

To complement your understanding of team—and specifically, your team's strengths and weaknesses, as well as your own personal strengths and weaknesses as a team member—the authors of Team Renaissance®: The Art, Science and Politics of Great Teams have developed two online assessment tools.

The first, a complementary assessment, is a simple question and answer session for individuals to use to learn more about ways to become better team players. The straightforward assessment categorizes each person into one of six roles on a team, offering an overview of what role a person plays on a team and how he or she is best able to make the most significant contributions in the structure of the team.

The second online assessment is more dynamic and is designed for each member of a team to take. After each member of the team has completed a 15-minute online assessment, the Team Assessment offers an in-depth look at the workings of the team—both perceived and real. The

Team Assessment helps identify where the weaknesses and perceived weaknesses of a team lie. Does a team struggle with sharp insights or in making handoffs? Does every team member truly understand the team's goals and objectives? Is email communication a bigger issue than the team leader realizes? Does the team follow through on its defined measures, or is it not using measures effectively? Is the team leader on the same page as the rest of the team?

The online mechanism is simple for both assessments. Go to www.teamrenaissance.net to register. The Team Assessment requires the team leader to sign up and register for one of the packages with a variety of options and deliverables. Registering a team to take the Team Assessment requires that the team leader have an email address for each team member. Before registering, the team leader should also advise team members to anticipate an email from Team Renaissance.

For best results, the authors and their team have learned that asking team members to take the online assessment within 24 hours of receiving the email works best.

Key performance indicators consistently link to exceptional team achievement as outlined in this book. The 15-minute Team Assessment will measure your team's input against the key performance indicators. Your feedback will then be merged with data from other members of your team. The consolidated information will lead to a better understanding of where your team falls short and what your team does well.

For more information about the team assessment, visit:

teamrenaissance.net

About the Authors and Contributors

Richard Spoon

Richard Spoon has done extensive work and consulting experience across North America and Europe. Prior to founding ArchPoint, he spent more than 15 years at Procter & Gamble and the Campbell Soup Company leading commercial organizations. Throughout his professional life, Richard has led large organization change efforts and worked with a diverse group of clients crossing continents, languages, industries, business size and functions. He is a frequent writer and speaker on topics related to business management, customer service, high performing organizations and continues his work leading organizational change. Richard received his MBA from the Kellogg School of Management at Northwestern University and a BBA from Texas State University. Richard resides with his wife and four children in Lafayette, Louisiana, where he is a Cub Scout Den Leader.

Jan Risher

Jan Risher grew up in a family full of storytellers in her native Mississippi. She went around the world to get from Mississippi to Louisiana—with stops in between ranging from the mountains of Slovakia, the streets of Paris, a tribal village in Burkina Faso to the hills of central Mexico. She's been a regular columnist for three newspapers and continues to write a Sunday column for Lafayette, Louisiana's *Daily Advertiser*. She is the former managing editor of The Times of Acadiana, and has been a full-time teacher and owner of a public relations firm. She continues a freelance writing career. She is a graduate of Mississippi State University.

Jesse Edelman

Jesse Edelman began his career with Procter & Gamble in IT, Sales Analytics and Category Management. Following P&G, Jesse had a variety of experiences ranging from Luke Soules/Acosta (Food Broker) to Webvan (e-tailer) to Heinz (Safeway Team Leader), to Senior Vice President of Sales for Jarden Home Brands, and finally as a Partner with The Partnering Group in the Sales and Marketing practice. He is a strong customer advocate to his clients helping them rethink their approach to service, markets, and business segments. Jesse received his Bachelor of Science from Rensselaer Polytechnic Institute.

Stephen Peele

Stephen Peele has more than 26 years of experience in high technology, information technology, and manufacturing products and services with GE, SmartSignal Corporation (a technology start-up) and independent consulting. His prior leadership positions include General Manager-Aviation at SmartSignal, E-Business Leader for GE Capital, Sales Director, Director of Marketing, and Director of New Business Development for GE Engine Services. Stephen earned an MBA from University of Cincinnati, a B.S. in Aeronautics and Astronautics from the Massachusetts Institute of Technology, and is certified in Six Sigma Quality and Continuous Improvement. He also currently serves as Adjunct Professor of Change Leadership at the Northern Kentucky University.

Index